UNITE Histc
Volume 2 (1932–1945)

The Transport and General Workers' Union (TGWU):
'No Turning Back': The Road to War and Welfare

UNITE History
Volume 2
(1932–1945)

The Transport and
General Workers' Union (TGWU):
'No Turning Back': The Road to War
and Welfare

Roger Seifert

LIVERPOOL UNIVERSITY PRESS

First published 2022 by
Liverpool University Press
4 Cambridge Street
Liverpool
L69 7ZU

Copyright © Marx Memorial Library & Workers' School (2022)

Roger Seifert has asserted the right to be identified as the author of this
book in accordance with the Copyright, Designs and Patents Act 1988.

British Library Cataloguing-in-Publication data
A British Library CIP record is available

ISBN 978-1-802-07698-1

Typeset by Carnegie Book Production, Lancaster
Printed and bound by CPI Group (UK) Ltd, Croydon CR0 4YY

Contents

Figures

Boxes

Acknowledgements

Graham Stevenson started researching and writing this volume. Sadly he died before he was able to complete his work. His family kindly allowed me to use some of his case studies. Ally Keane and Mark Metcalf from the North East regional group provided me with a raft of excellent material which I have used throughout. Others who assisted are acknowledged along the way. Tom Sibley and John Foster provided helpful comments on earlier drafts.

Abbreviations

ATGWU	Amalgamated Transport and General Workers' Union
BBC	British Broadcasting Corporation
BDC	Biennial Delegate Conference
BMA	British Medical Association
BUF	British Union of Fascists
CP	Communist Party
CPGB	Communist Party of Great Britain
GC	General Council
GEC	General Executive Committee
GS	General Secretary
EC	Executive Committee
FBI	Federation of British Industry
IB	International Brigade
IER	Institute of Employment Rights
ILO	International Labour Organisation
IMF	International Monetary Fund
IRA	Irish Republican Army
ITGWU	Irish Transport and General Workers' Union
JIC	Joint Industrial Council
JPC	Joint Production Committee
LCC	London County Council
LP	Labour Party
MFGB	Miners Federation of Great Britain
MP	Member of Parliament
NEC	National Executive Committee
NCLC	National Council of Labour Colleges
NUGM	National Union of General and Municipal Workers
NUWM	National Unemployed Workers Movement
PLP	Parliamentary Labour Party
RTC	Road Transport Commercial
RTP	Road Transport Passenger

SL	Socialist League
STUC	Scottish Trade Union Congress
TC	Trades Council
TGWU	Transport and General Workers' Union
TUC	Trades Union Congress
USA	United States of America
USSR	Union of Soviet Socialist Republics
UK	United Kingdom
WEA	Workers' Education Association
WETUC	Workers' Educational Trade Union Committee

Foreword

Unite History Project
The Six-Volume History

2022 marks the centenary of the formation of the Transport & General Workers' Union (T&G), now a part of Unite, Britain and Ireland's largest union in private industry. The T&G was also a significant workers' organisation in public-sector employment, a tradition carried forward into Unite.

The T&G was the first general trade union, taking pride in organising workers in every occupation and delivering collective bargaining across a multitude of industries. The T&G held real industrial power through much of its history, and it was from this basis that millions of working people won better pay and conditions that dramatically improved living standards.

The union also exercised a great deal of political influence, particularly within the Labour Party. This and its interaction with government, often as a powerful independent actor in its own right, provide the setting for a wider chronological history of the labour movement in Britain – and to that extent also the industrial and political history of Britain; it was not without a significant impact in Ireland as well.

This history reflects and exposes the wider processes of social change in which working people played an active role, in terms of creating an understanding of oppression in society and exploitation, particularly of women and black people, in the workplace. In addition, the union's international work and campaigns are brought into sharp focus.

Many of the T&G's general secretaries, from Bevin to Morris, have been the subject of biographies, and Jack Jones published an autobiography. But this series is different: among other things it examines how the union's central function, campaigning and winning on jobs, pay and conditions, evolved over the course of the twentieth century.

This six-volume series tells this story in a highly original way, as it enables the incorporation of local history as played out by the union's shop stewards and branch officers. Work has been undertaken at regional level, based on interviews and newly uncovered archival material, that brings our history to life and gives a human dimension to an otherwise 'top level' narrative. Unions are after all composed of individuals – in the T&G's case, hundreds of thousands.

I believe that these volumes will make a great contribution to Unite's educational programmes with its members, workplace representatives and other activists, and more generally in colleges and universities; nothing like this work has been published before.

If we are to avoid the mistakes of the past it is of course essential that we understand and learn from it! This series of six books, detailing the history of one of the twentieth century's most important and vital trade unions, gives us that opportunity, and I commend them to you.

Sharon Graham
General Secretary
Unite the Union

I

Trade Unionism in the 'Age of Catastrophe' (1931–1939)

The more workers know of their history, the more resolute, and the better able, they will be to make history today.[1]

From its foundation the T&G has played a leading part in the wider labour movement. Its history is inseparable from that of the whole trade union movement and of the Labour Party.[2]

1 A.J. Cook, 'Foreword' to *The Miners' Struggle* by John Hammond (Plebs League, 1926), p.1.
2 'The History of the T&G', *Unite the Union* (website).

Introduction

This is the story of working-class power exercised through trade unions. Power gained through struggle, organization, and relevance; power used through negotiations, strikes, and political impact; and power defended against attacks by Conservatives in government, by so-called friends inside the labour movement, and by those sections of opinion formers (the media, academics, church leaders) seeking to sow doubt and division. Mass unemployment undermined that power. It meant terrible hardships for those involved, it meant wasted talent, and it cast a long dark shadow over working-class lives. It undermined the bargaining power of those in work, and it reduced union effectiveness. It created conditions that allowed some workers to be tempted by the siren voices of the fascists. It helped to divide and rule as the class struggle intensified across communities.

The main themes discussed here include the Transport and General Workers Union (TGWU)'s collective bargaining strategy based on the fight for official, formal national agreements; the growth of the union as a priority to fulfil these aims; and how members, through area and industrial sections, could remain inside the TGWU while facing different challenges. Such achievements depended on forcing through relationships with the state that benefited such a strategy. That required a strong central leader, absence of dissent, and a political disposition that favoured deals with big business and co-operation in tripartite institutions.

In 1932, ten years after the founding of the TGWU, the union remained a large and rambling organization. It was dominated by its powerful general secretary, Ernest Bevin (officially in office 1922–1946).[3] The majority of

---

3 Alan Bullock, *The Life and Times of Ernest Bevin, Trade Union Leader 1881–1940* (Heinemann, 1960); Alan Bullock, *The Life and Times of Ernest Bevin, Minister of Labour 1940–1945* (Heinemann, 1967); for an infantile view see Andrew Adonis, *Ernest Bevin: Labour's Churchill* (Biteback, 2020); for a more critical appreciation, Peter Weiler, *Ernest Bevin* (Manchester University Press, 1993).

its General Executive Committee (GEC) and officials were supporters of his approach to industrial relations, trade unionism, and wider labour movement politics. Since the start the TGWU members had witnessed, in quick succession, the 1926 General Strike, the 1927–1928 Mond-Turner talks, the 1929 Great Crash, and the chronic failure of the minority Labour governments of 1924 and 1929–1931.

The Great Depression wrecked the social order, destroyed communities, and cast doubt on the efficacy of capitalism and its traditional remedies. Leaders of those nations with relatively short existences and weak national identities (Italy and Germany) were creating fake histories and symbols to establish credible claims to political power beyond the rule of law. Cultural technologies, such as radio and cinema, allowed mass (mis)information on an unknown scale, and with that came the call for national salvation and a new world order – fascists and Nazis.

In 1932 the peoples of Europe were faced with a new set of related crises. It had only been 13 years after the brutal murder of Rosa Luxemburg, 14 years since the end of the First World War with the Spanish flu pandemic, 15 years since the Russian Revolution, and 16 years from the cruel execution of James Connolly.[4] The 1929 Wall Street crash led to mass unemployment in Europe and America.[5] In all of this, men and women went about their lives at work (some in new factories and offices), at home (with new domestic appliances), in leisure activities (in cars and on holiday), and in political, social, and religious gatherings (fuelled now by mass literacy, newspapers, and the ubiquitous wireless). Traditional beliefs were uprooted and re-rooted in different forms, old certainties were questioned, and familiar paths to a better life closed down. Mass unemployment scarred the nation. While the great global movements were pushing and shoving peoples across the continents, individual lives were being played out in real time against great injustice and uncertainty.

The 1930s was a decade of heightened struggle in every realm of existence: work and home, family and community, science and technology, culture and religion, politics and ideologies, and trade unions. The battle for political ideas and ideals was fought in thousands of workplaces and union branches, and so the tale of the TGWU members and activists is part of the story of British life. Once the war started in 1939, until its end in 1945, workers and their unions were still involved in the familiar battles of the class, and old antagonisms were on display even during such a national effort.

4 Rosa Luxemburg (1871–1919) was a communist revolutionary murdered by German Nazis. James Connolly (1868–1916) was an Irish trade union leader and revolutionary who led the Dublin Easter Rising and was executed by the British army.

5 J.K. Galbraith, *The Great Crash, 1929* (Penguin, 1954).

The Russian Revolution was a major factor. It inspired many working-class activists to form communist parties (CPs), become socialists, lead struggles, and fight for a better world. Its impact on British workers was immense, but it also unleashed a backlash of anti-communism that became the marking stone of much of the politics of the 1930s. This was sharper after the Great Crash seemed to have vindicated the Marxist analysis that capitalism was unstable, unconvincing, and ready to be overthrown. The anti-communists, especially in the British trade union movement, were prepared to go to great lengths to reduce and eliminate communist influence, and Bevin at the TGWU and Walter Citrine at the Trades Union Congress (TUC) were at the helm of this anti-red crusade.[6] In the UK, as in the USA, 'the formation of the first socialist government [USSR] thrilled and inspired [...] radicals'.[7] Soviet communism became the only really existing alternative to capitalism, and as such those adherents of Marxism-Leninism became the enemy of both the capitalist class and those in the labour movement seeking to reform and refresh capitalist society from within.

This history illustrates the famous dictum that while women and men make their own history, they do not do so under circumstances of their own choosing. Here the workers' tale is told through the prism of the TGWU in this 'age of catastrophe'.[8]

The labour movement seemed lost as the national government on 27 October 1931 decisively won the general election headed by the Labour leader Ramsey MacDonald. It was a landslide election victory for the national government which won 67 per cent of the votes and 554 seats (470 of them Conservatives). The Labour Party suffered its greatest defeat, losing four out of five of its seats. The Liberal Party split into three factions and continued to shrink. Later the Conservatives easily won the 1935 election under Stanley Baldwin. Such massive parliamentary wins hid the truth of the matter, and helped to nourish the seeds, already sown, of a revanchist Labour Party, labour and trade union movement, and the varied calls of the socialist and communist wings of the international.

The TGWU was celebrating its tenth anniversary in 1932 when the economic and industrial slump was reaping its bitter harvest. Bevin felt that the 'amalgamation has been fully justified' but that at present we need 'a grim, determined effort' to see off the attacks from employers (*The Record*, January 1932).

6 Walter Citrine, *Men and Work* (Hutchinson, 1964); Walter Citrine, *Two Careers* (Hutchinson, 1967); Jim Moher, *Walter Citrine: Forgotten Statesman of the Trades Union Congress* (JGM Books, 2021).

7 Philip Foner, *The Bolshevik Revolution: Its Impact on American Radicals, Liberals, and Labor* (International Publishers, 1967), p.20.

8 Eric Hobsbawm, *Age of Extremes: The Short Twentieth Century 1914–1991* (Michael Joseph, 1994).

What Is Trade Unionism, and the Legacy of the 1926 General Strike

A trade union is: 'a continuous association of wage earners for the purpose of maintaining or improving the conditions of their working lives'.[9] Furthermore, it was the impulse which came from

> the miseries and disorders, the increase in class antagonisms, the stirring of new ideas, which accompanied the revolutionary wars after 1789 and the use of steam-power and the factory system. For the first time political and industrial ideas began powerfully to interact; the struggle for parliamentary reform became inextricably interwoven with the desperate fight of miners and factory operatives against the oppression of the new industrial order.[10]

In Bevin's view

> the primary function of the union is service; negotiating wage changes and improvements in hours; attending to legal and unemployment claims; and obtaining various orders for the protection of life and limb, protecting working people against dismissals, and, day in day out, watching with close interest the needs of the membership. (*The Record*, June 1932)

In 1938 G.D.H. Cole undertook a survey of trade unionism which made clear that the quietism of the trade union leadership throughout the 1930s was rooted in the 'sorry business' of the 1926 General Strike. He goes on 'it provided, indeed, a magnificent display of working-class solidarity [...] from the standpoint of the Trade Union rank and file, the General Strike was carried out with exemplary courage and loyalty', but there was total lack of leadership from the TUC's General Council (GC) – no preparation, no plan, and no idea of how to deal with the government once their bluff had been called. As a result 'the outcome was deep and bitter disillusionment'. Members left unions and activists lost heart. The real meaning of the subsequent Mond-Turner pact was for the employers to incorporate trade unions into the capitalist machine from a position of humble weakness. 'The Trades Union Congress, cowed and financially prostrate as a result of the General Strike, accepted these recommendations by a large majority' only opposed by A.J. Cook of the miners and a few other left-wingers. Ever since the 1931 defeat of the Labour government, the trade union leaders have acted in the spirit of Mond's proposals. Cole

---

9 Sidney and Beatrice Webb, *The History of Trade Unionism* (Longman, 1920), p.1.
10 G.D.H. Cole, *Organised Labour* (George Allen and Unwin, 1924), pp.1–2.

concludes: 'It [the TUC] has endeavoured, not to challenge capitalism, but to make terms with it; and it has regarded as its worst enemies, not the employers, but those Trade Unionists who have endeavoured to recall it to a more militant policy'.[11] This became the calling card of the majority of the TGWU's leaders throughout the 1930s.

It was this class-on-class infighting that was the badge that defined British working-class struggle throughout the 1930s: pro-capitalist right-wing social democrats versus the array of socialists and communists, sometimes under the Marxist mantra, but always anti-capitalist. The leadership of the TGWU was clearly on one side of this schism, and not just as spectators but as major cheer leaders.

The number of unions fell from 1,081 in 1932 to 781 by 1945. Over the same period their membership rose from a total of 4,444,000 to 7,875,000. This was evidence for Bevin's view that big was better. The financial importance of unions was evident with total funds for all registered unions rising from £11,192,000 to £42,417,000. This underlined the need, already recognized by the TGWU leaders, of centralized administrative and financial control and probity.[12]

Bevin bestrode the TGWU like a modern day Ozymandias, and played a major part in both the TUC and Labour Party during these years. His dominance is reflected in his control over the TGWU's monthly journal, *The Record* – 'a journal devoted to the interests of all transport and general workers'. In his own way Bevin came to the conclusion that: 'the security for wages lies in increased capital and the enlargement of enterprise'.[13] Such a sentiment allowed Bevin to see the benefits of the power of large trade unions making terms with ever-larger firms and more state intervention. This partly accounts for his drive to secure increased membership, his desire to be part of the power brokerage system in the country for the benefit of workers, and to fight off any disrupting influences – especially communists – from inside the union.

The TGWU's collective bargaining strategy was founded on formal recognition by employers and the drive for national and binding agreements. This helped the weak but hindered the strong. National agreements in hard-to-organize sectors kept wages higher than otherwise, but it also tended to keep wages lower where the members were strongly organized and willing to fight.

11   G.D.H. Cole, *British Trade Unionism Today* (Methuen, 1939), pp.73–77.
12   Thanks to Ben Seifert for collecting the data.
13   Dyer Lum, *Philosophy of Trade Unions: An Essay Devoted to the Interests of the Thousands Who, in the Daily Struggle for Labor's Rights, Do Battle for the True Freedom of the Human Race* (American Federation of Labor, 1892), p.19.

The Great Depression: 'Brother, Can You Spare a Dime?'[14]

The 1930s were dominated by the state of the economy.[15] There was slow growth until 1934, low inflation, steady wage increases for those in work after 1935, large-scale unemployment until 1936, and significant sectoral and regional variations. The industrial heartlands were hardest hit while London and the Midlands experienced rapid growth. All of this had an impact directly and indirectly upon the trade union movement, and in particular on TGWU members. UK economic growth remained uneven ranging from -4.97 per cent in 1931 to 6.21 per cent in 1934, slipping back again to 0.66 per cent in 1938 but recovering quickly to 4.64 per cent by 1939.

The debate on the causes of the economic crash raged across orthodoxies as blows were traded between those concerned with demand-side economics and those wedded to the supply side. This mattered since the remedies were partly rooted in perceived causes, and the capitalist system itself came under hostile attack. Some economists came down firmly on the demand side, arguing that real wages followed a path consistent with 'demand shocks and import price movements'.[16]

The government came under great pressure as both the financial markets and the 'real economy' deteriorated. With record levels of unemployment and growing social unrest there was the familiar tension between fiscal probity by cutting spending, and borrowing to spend. The former won the day and the Labour leaders infamously led a national government that cut benefits and reduced wages. In 1932 the bank rate was cut and this allowed interest rates to fall, thereby cheapening the cost of borrowing linked with quitting the gold standard.[17] The pound fell by 28 per cent against the dollar.

This monetary policy enabled an increase in the money supply of 34 per cent between 1932 and 1936, and there was an increase in private sector investment and consumption. The rates of economic growth from 1934 were reasonable, and there was a significant fall in the official national insurance-based estimates of unemployment from 22.1 per cent in 1932 to 10.5 per cent in 1938, and again to 1.3 per cent by the end of the war in 1945. Area variations were significant with, for example, London ranging from 12.9 per cent in 1932 falling to 7.4 per cent by 1939. In contrast, Wales fell from 36.8 per cent to 22 per cent, Scotland from 28.2 per cent to 16.1 per cent, and the North East from 28.8 per cent to 11.8 per cent over

---

14 Written in 1932 for the musical *Americana* by the socialist songwriter Yip Harburg.

15 Summary by economicshelp.org.

16 N.H. Dimsdale, S.J. Nickell, and N. Horsewood, 'Real Wages and Unemployment in Britain during the 1930s', *The Economic Journal*, 1989, vol.99, no.396, pp.271–292.

17 The gold standard is when a country's currency is convertible into gold.

the same time. In the late 1930s, a gradual rearmament programme began a belated fiscal stimulus. This provided an additional boost to demand and economic growth, but full employment only returned by 1941.

Outline of This Volume

Part I of this volume includes a discussion of unemployment, the influence of Mondism on the TGWU's productivity bargaining strategy, and the tensions between the official TGWU position and the rank and file. This is most starkly portrayed in disputes over speed-up – management practices, mainly in factories, of increasing the rate of work. As the 1930s progressed there was some industrial growth in London and the Midlands around building and engineering. Developments among dockers, road hauliers, and London busmen are covered, alongside the special case of the TGWU in Ireland, and its status among women workers. All this is set against the backdrop of the rise of fascism and Nazism at home and abroad with the tragic unfolding of the Spanish Civil War.

The TGWU leadership, dominated by Bevin, sought to build the union as a centralized force side by side with the increasingly important TUC having a real impact in both the industrial and political worlds. The main strategy was to formalize collective bargaining within national frameworks under the control of the appointed union officials. This push took place differently for each sector, but the overall aim was to force employers to bargain and to enlist government support if and when possible. Underlining this position was the notion that a reformed and modernized capitalist economy could benefit both the workers and the nation, and the job of the unions was to help secure this more efficient rationalization. Those guilty of disruption, especially communist-dominated rank-and-file movements, were to be attacked and expelled.

Part II covers the approach of war with an economic recovery. The political schisms intensified and TGWU members faced a range of new management initiatives partly secured through negotiated agreements. During the war, strikes were outlawed, and workers went either to fight or were redeployed through industrial conscription. Women entered the workforce in greater numbers, and unions joined with employers to form joint production committees on the ground and be part of national arrangements for labour, and with Bevin now Minister of Labour, the TGWU became the dominate union in the land.

As the war progressed to its climax, so anti-communism and anti-Sovietism were in abeyance. Post-war plans for reconstruction were gaining popular support with demands for full employment, national insurance and health provision, universal education, and state ownership of key industries. This went with a determination to prevent both a return to the pre-war slump, and to stop the working classes from bearing the brunt of the war effort. The new world order under US control saw the British Empire about to gasp its last sigh.

1

'Journeys through Hell'[1]

Introduction

Between the election of the national government in September 1931 and the resounding victory of the Conservatives in the election of November 1935, the people of Great Britain experienced large-scale unemployment, witnessed the rise of fascism, and were fed a diet of raw anti-communism. The TGWU survived through a mixture of official policies on the establishment of formal collective bargaining machinery, and the militancy of rank-and-file activists in the workplaces. Concession bargaining became the common currency of the TGWU in these years of political defeat and economic recession. This chapter covers such matters, while the next chapter details some of the main sectional developments inside the union.

September 1931 was the watershed of the interwar years. It marked the end of the gold standard, it witnessed the Japanese invasion of Manchuria, Mussolini's fascists had been in government for nearly a decade, popular sentiment turned away from monarchy and Empire, and there was the rise and rise of domestic goods through the wonders of hire purchase. It also marked a remarkable conversion of sorts to planning (of sorts): a planned economy, a plan for peace, planned families, planned holidays, and plans to revive older industrial towns and regions while those workers that could were leaving them anyway.

The 1931 general election was fought on the major promise to save the pound and balance the budget. A.J.P. Taylor wryly notes: 'a crisis of muddle which no one properly understood led to a general election of unrivalled confusion'.[2] It showed the once dominant Liberals in retreat and

---

1 Alan Sillitoe (1964) uses this phrase to sum up the tales told in Robert Tressell's *The Ragged Trousered Philanthropists* (c.1914).

2 A.J.P. Taylor, *English History, 1914–1945* (Clarendon Press, 1965), p.321.

exposed the bitter divisions inside the Labour Party. While the old familiar of free trade versus protectionism loomed large in the debates inside Parliament, outside the dominant concern was unemployment. The TUC and individual trade unions had lost faith in the Parliamentary Labour Party (PLP) under George Lansbury, and began to pin their hopes on two rising stars: Clement Attlee and Stafford Cripps.

There were about 45 million citizens living in Britain, with a low birth rate and therefore low population growth.[3] Motor transport in the shape of buses (more used than trains) and cars (doubled in number to two million by 1938) began to enable the rapid growth in new housing and new factories, increasing out-of-town centres and markets, hence the rise and rise of London, Manchester, Cardiff, Glasgow, and Birmingham. The economic recovery started with car manufacture and housebuilding, and by 1934 had spread to hotels, restaurants, and general entertainment – all signs of greater prosperity among some sections. By 1939 over 11 million workers had paid holiday leave and used it to venture forth.

This had an impact on the industrial composition of the labour force, for example, with more clerical and administrative workers alongside the rise of the semi-skilled factory operatives. This in turn shifted the balance of membership and power within the trade union movement. The diverse and scattered membership of the TGWU shared some of this sense of being 'better off' with more to have and to hold. Much was being cemented socially and politically through the wonders of radio and the increasing role of the British Broadcasting Corporation (BBC) in everyday lives. Alongside the spoken word came the mass circulation of newspapers benefitting from near universal literacy.

The Times, Mail, Telegraph, and Daily Express catered for aspirational and actual Tories. The Daily Herald along with the Daily Mirror was the paper of choice for labour supporters, and the former played its part in the development of the movement with the more intellectual and liberal New Statesman dominated by J.M. Keynes and Kingsley Martin. The Daily Worker was the paper for the most advanced sections of the trade union and socialist movement. The so-called press barons, such as Beaverbrook and Rothermere, owned nearly half of all print news, while the worker-centred press had to rely on its readers and supporters for funding.

In the cinema the triumph of the talkies and the hegemonic grip of Hollywood brought untold thrills to a large section of the more mobile working classes. Laurel and Hardy poked endless fun at the fault lines in the American dream. This was accompanied by the growth in sporting events across the board (horse and dog racing, tennis, football, rugby,

---

3 Noreen Branson and Margot Heinemann, *Britain in the Nineteen Thirties* (Panther, 1973), pp.180–185.

and cricket); the rise of the thriller novel with its greatest exponent Agatha Christie, and the more select but highly influential literary world of Virginia Woolf, alongside W.H. Auden and Christopher Isherwood, and Daphne du Maurier. The trade union and labour movement were caught up in these changes and required to rethink the ways in which they communicated their ideas to their cohorts, to restructure their organizations to match the more flexible development of industrial sectors and skills, to accept changes within the labour force, and ultimately to recast their policy programmes and political priorities to fit the new Britain. The TGWU leadership, while slow to recognize some of these trends, nonetheless managed, through the trade group system, to satisfy 'the aspirations for self-determination of the heterogeneous general workers'.[4]

At this time the TGWU was divided into 13 geographical areas and eight main trade groups, the largest of which were in the docks and waterways, transport (both passenger and commercial), and the catch-all of general workers. It forged a collective bargaining strategy based on formal national agreements where possible. This required both an ideological and practical accommodation with large employers and employer federations within the orbit of a more interventionist government. As a result there were significant tensions between the 'official line' and the unofficial movements, and this led to infighting and unofficial strikes.

The TUC assumed a larger role in both the life of the labour movement and the country as a whole. It was dominated by the large unions, especially the Miners' Federation of Great Britain (MFGB), alongside the two growing general unions, the National Union of General and Municipal Workers (NUGM) and the TGWU. The TGWU leadership forged a powerful alliance with the TUC's general secretary, Citrine. Together they pushed a hard agenda of compromise with employers, dealings with government if and when possible, trade union growth through improved administration and tight central controls, and a fierce anti-communism at home and abroad. Coates and Topham claim that

> [u]nder the leadership of Walter Citrine (General Secretary) and Ernest Bevin of the TGWU, the TUC in the interwar and war years pursued a constitutional role, and continued the historical trend towards a wider involvement in consultations with governments, and participation in the affairs of state as a very junior partner.[5]

4 Vic Allen, *Trade Union Leadership: Based on a Study of Arthur Deakin* (Longmans Green, 1957), p.155.
5 Ken Coates and Tony Topham, *Trade Unions in Britain* (Fontana, 1988), p.111.

The Bevin Supremacy

In August 1931 the minority Labour government was failing. The TGWU made it clear that this was a financial crisis, and that the TUC had to stay firm in its resolve that the burden of the crisis must not land at the door of the working classes. The TGWU took the view that cuts to benefits were indeed an attack on both workers and the labour movement. Meetings with the dying government did nothing to change their minds and thus they opposed the plans for wage and benefit cuts. As Bevin stated 'the trade union movement must go on doing its duty [...] [because] cuts in unemployment benefit are a prelude to cuts in wages' (*The Record*, September 1931).

After the 1931 general election, the TGWU's GEC bitterly opposed the formation and direction of the new national government. Bevin saw what was coming as he possessed, 'the prophetic touch of imagination, that sense of historical change'.[6] The TGWU was hampered by the election of the national government with its economic policies based on laissez-faire, its politics based on ruling class elitism, and its social and cultural attitudes steeped in imperial privilege and colonial entitlement. Nonetheless, even this reactionary set of leaders could not hold back the powerful tide of capitalist dynamism, and the aspirations of an increasingly restless working class. In such circumstances the Labour Party found itself once again unsure how to blend and mend its socialist rhetoric with its social democratic instincts.

Throughout the 1930s the TGWU, the TUC and trades councils (TCs), the Labour Party (LP) and wider labour movement were beset by divisions. They came together on some issues and fell apart on others. Finding a way through the complexities of everyday working life set against the backdrop of recession, impending war, and the rise of fascism, was always for debate. Tactics come and go, strategic interests can be hard to see in the fog of union struggles, but a clarity of analysis and purpose was forged by some. The divisions can be crystalized as between social democrats and the left socialist-CP axis. The former opposed fascism and communism with equal vigour, favoured a Mondist approach to collective bargaining based on accommodation with employers, and turned their backs on the United Front and the National Unemployed Workers' Movement (NUWM). In contrast, the latter group were unrelentingly anti-fascist, supported rank-and-file struggles, and backed the United Front and NUWM. The rest of this chapter follows these splits over unemployment, collective bargaining, and local strikes.

The centre of the class struggle shifted to the trade unions. Other than in the cotton industry (with the strike by weavers in 1932) there were no

6 Bullock, *Trade Union Leader*, p.494.

major strikes sanctioned by the leadership. It became a 'soldiers' war' – a fight from below against cuts to benefits, against unemployment, and against pay cuts and job losses.[7] From 1933–1939 there were 735 strikes recorded involving 295,000 workers with 1,694,000 striker days. This last figure measures the length of disputes and the numbers involved, and was the lowest for any period between 1900 and 1970. Importantly it was far lower in every regard than the previous decade and shows the extent to which widespread worker militancy was diminished by the combination of unemployment and political defeat.[8]

Once the 1931 election was over the employers queued up to demand wage cuts. TGWU members across sectors from seed crushing to paint, colour, and varnish were faced with pay cuts. The members opposed them naturally, but the union insisted upon constitutional deals through the relevant Joint Industrial Councils (JICs). It agreed pay cuts for gas and electricity staff. In some sectors – shipbuilding and repairs – cuts were imposed by the employers. Indeed, employers forced through pay cuts by threatening to walk away from collective bargaining arrangements. This was a dagger at the heart of the TGWU's strategy since formal participation in constitutional bodies was the centrepiece of its policy (*The Record*, November 1931). The TGWU official line was that some of these wage cuts were 'a fairly good settlement' (*The Record*, December 1931, about dockers).

Bevin's negotiating skills were frequently praised on the basis that he had managed to reduce wage cuts without resorting to strike action. This is a naïve view of negotiations. It would be a terrible union negotiator who could not shift an employer from their opening demands. The TGWU EC supported accommodation with big business and the TUC's position of 'supporting rationalisation of industries'.[9] While attacking crude versions of speed-up, such as the Bedaux system, the TGWU sought to negotiate through its imposition rather than oppose outright. Such productivity-style bargaining, mooted in the Mond-Turner talks, became the centrepiece of the TGWU's industrial relations' policy. Exploitation was to be moderated but not abolished.

This is the core of the case: 'an old fallacy was refurbished in the suggestion that increased production was the gateway to working-class prosperity [...] rationalisation of industry was viewed not as a process of intensification of labour through speed-up, mechanisation, etc., but as 'a more efficient, economical and humane system of production', as Bevin said at the 1929 TUC conference in Belfast.[10]

7 Allen Hutt, *The Post-War History of the British Working Class* (Victor Gollancz, 1937), pp.214–243.
8 Richard Hyman, *Strikes* (Fontana, 1972), pp.26–27.
9 A.J. Cook, *The Mond Moonshine* (Workers' Publication, c.1928), p.9.
10 Allen Hutt, *British Trade Unionism: A Short History, 1800–1961* (Lawrence & Wishart, 1962), p.120.

After the 1931 Bristol conference the TUC began a more constructive relationship with the Labour Party leadership. They understood that the level of unemployment benefit was directly linked with wage negotiations. While there was backing for forms of public ownership they were uninterested in worker control, but John Cliff of the TGWU moved that under public ownership workers, through their union representatives, should have 'an adequate and direct share in the control and administration of such industry or service'.[11] The TGWU leaders urged their members to vote Labour and became more active in Labour Party affairs. They had no doubt that the national government 'have used their power, not in saving the country from financial crisis, but in creating an economic crisis in the homes of the British working class' (*The Record*, October 1931).

At the 1932 TUC Newcastle conference, Harold Clay of the TGWU, with Bevin's support, wanted worker representation on boards, foreshadowing Joint Production Committees (JPCs) set up during the war. Unemployment was the main concern both in itself and more particularly because it meant falling union membership. The TGWU turned its back on any radical opposition and especially the NUWM. 'The problem was of course communism',[12] and a deputation from the NUWM was refused entry to congress. The mood was depressed and depressing.

The other row which showed Bevin's darker side was an attack on communists seeking to stir up opposition to Japanese incursions into China. The CP called upon dockers to stop the transportation of munitions, but Bevin won the day, showering the idea with cold water and hot rhetoric. Yet within a year Hitler had come to power, and even the TUC had to take note. In 1932 there was an inter-organizational arrangement that allowed Bevin and the TGWU more say in the political arena: the setting up of the National Joint Council (later the National Council of Labour). Bevin staunchly protested against the socialist and socializing mood from the floor of the Labour Party's 1932 conference in Leicester. He was unhappy with delegates' insistence that the next Labour government 'must nationalize the joint stock banks as well as the Bank of England, and must set out upon an immediate programme of constructive Socialism'.[13]

In March 1933 both the TUC GC and the Labour Party National Executive Committee rejected calls for a 'united labour' front against fascism. The TGWU denounced Hitler's attacks on German trade unionists and social democrats, and blamed a lack of left unity for his rise to power. The union argued that 'there was nothing to be gained by

11 John Lovell and Ben Roberts, *A Short History of the TUC* (MacMillan, 1968), p.125.
12 Lovell and Roberts, *TUC*, p.129.
13 G.D.H. Cole and Raymond Postgate, *The Common People 1746–1946* (Methuen, 1946), p.598.

mere denunciation of Hitler' (*The Record*, May 1933). Since the TGWU leadership also blamed the communists, they were unable to provide 'unity' themselves.

Oswald Moseley's black shirts had started the British campaign for fascism which provoked the rise of anti-fascism as a core element of left-wing activity. The National Council for Civil Liberties (now known as Liberty) was founded in 1934 just for that purpose. Also:

> In 1933, the fiftieth anniversary of the death of Karl Marx, a delegate meeting comprising trade unionists, veteran social-ists belonging to the Labour Party and Communist Party, and representatives of the Labour Research Department and Martin Lawrence Publishers Ltd., considered setting up a permanent memorial to him. That year also saw the Nazis in Germany burning books. In these circumstances the meeting resolved that the most appropriate memorial would be a Library. Thus the Marx Memorial Library and Workers School was established at 37a Clerkenwell Green that year. (Marx Memorial Library website)

Bevin's anti-communism was not just a form of labour imperialism, it was rooted in his strong belief that for the TGWU to succeed it had to be centrally controlled. The main thorn in the leadership's side was the London busmen, for unlike the TGWU, the other general union, the NUGM, 'had solved the problem of Communist influence by simply banning their election to union office – a drastic measure which may have been facili-tated by the strength of Irish Catholicism within the membership'.[14] When in 1932 and again in 1933 the London busmen fought against wage cuts through their own organization, the Rank-and-File Movement, the TGWU leadership turned on its own activists and members.[15]

With Hitler now in power in Germany, the sharp focus of the British labour movement was how best to fight fascism at home and abroad. Bevin and the TGWU leadership took a decisive wrong turn at the Biennial Delegate Conference (BDC) in the summer of 1933 when it failed to support the United Front (*The Record*, July and August 1933). The *Daily Worker* (12 July 1933) makes it clear:

> when Hitler become Chancellor, that unity and strength of the workers which can destroy Fascism had been weakened and split [...] this argument of Bevin's is designed to cover up the role of the German reformist trade unions in basely surrendering to Hitler [...] It is also designed to hide the fact that the British

14 Henry Pelling, *A History of British Trade Unionism* (Penguin, 1976), p.205.
15 Ken Fuller, *Radical Aristocrats: London Busworkers from the 1880s to the 1980s* (Lawrence & Wishart, 1985).

reformist leaders have not only refused to participate in the
united front against Fascism in Britain, but are doing [...] nothing
whatever to rally the masses.

Meanwhile Bevin was consolidating his grip on the higher echelons
of the union. Arthur Deakin (officially general secretary 1946–1955) was
the most important of these – a steel worker who had built the membership in North Wales, and moved from national secretary to assistant
general secretary (1934), and then in 1940 acting general secretary. With
Andrew Dalgleish running the new metal, engineering and chemical
group, the union position in the Midlands and car sector was firmly
established. By the 1932 conference TGWU membership was down to
373,000, continuing its fall since 1929. From 1933 onwards membership and income rose steadily (*The Record*, July/August 1933). During
the recession it became more difficult to recruit and organize. In some
areas local activity allowed for limited inroads even among hard-to-
reach groups such as road maintenance workers, brewery staff, and wire
workers at the Derby Cable Company in Long Eaton. Less success was
to be had in the efforts to gain a foothold among agricultural workers,
and this group remained in thrall to powerful employers throughout the
1930s despite the occasional union breakthrough.

The Brighton TUC in September 1933 and the Hastings conference
of Labour in October both argued at the same time to condemn Nazism
and oppose war preparations. More prosaically the Labour Party's report,
Socialism and the Condition of the People, debated trade union representation on the boards of nationalized industries.[16]

Bevin generally had no time for so-called intellectuals in the movement.
He saw them as unreliable and irresponsible. His time as chair of the Society
for Socialist Inquiry and Propaganda, which was founded by G.D.H. Cole,
Clement Attlee, Stafford Cripps, Raymond Postgate, and the left lawyer
D.N. Pritt, convinced him not to trust such left-thinking comrades. The
experience persuaded him of both the necessity for a political role for the
trade unions, and of the need to keep Marxists at bay.[17]

This was to some extent another of Bevin's masks to hide his devout
anti-communism and suspicions that the militants in his own union might
expose his endless compromises as, sometimes, just concession bargaining.
Bevin had the qualities of a 'prize fighter and a tragedian'.[18] He was the
authentic face of the English working classes, warts and all. His real
influence came from his ability to convince the powerful office holders

---

16 *Socialism and the Condition of the People*, report from the 1933 Labour Party
conference.

17 Weiler, *Bevin*, pp.63–68.

18 Bullock, *Trade Union Leader*, p.534.

in the Labour Party that he was the guardian of British trade unionism. As such he stood for 'law and order' inside the TGWU and the wider movement, and this allowed some semblance of justification for attacks on his own militants.

The specifics of the London busmen are dealt with later, but as an example of the TGWU leadership's opposition to dissent it is instructive. In the autumn of 1933 the TGWU Executive sent out an ultimatum to rank-and-file leaders, such as Bernard Sharkey, to dissociate themselves from the rank-and-file movement or be suspended from office. In November 1933 Bevin sued the *Daily Worker* for libel concerning the paper's accusations that he acted undemocratically against the busmen's rank-and-file group. He won £7,000 in compensation (*The Record*, December 1933). Reports of the case centred on Bevin's claims that strike calls by the group were 'irresponsible' and that he regarded the busmen's rank and file as a 'Communist cell in our movement'.

While the TGWU leaders were keen anti-communists, they were undoubtedly anti-fascist as well because, as they witnessed, 'trade unions were almost the first institutions to be smashed by the fascists'.[19] In February 1934 the Austrian government unleashed its own forces against the union movement. The TGWU launched a support campaign for their trade union comrades being attacked by fascists throughout Europe (*The Record*, February 1934). At last the official labour movement was stirred and started to fund anti-fascist propaganda. In their own backyard Moseley's black shirts were rousing fascist sentiments in Britain. The TGWU launched a counteroffensive using all their communication avenues in the fight back.

The 1934 TUC at Weymouth was held there in honour of the centenary of the Tolpuddle martyrs. Here was the start of the turn away from peace at any price, and towards preparation for war through rearmament. The Tolpuddle anniversary was used to launch a mass recruitment campaign and was the occasion for the play by Miles Malleson, *The Six Men of Dorset*. It ends with George Loveless talking with his wife, 'What we did was right, Betsy. I know that. That's somethin' [...] but I be tired [...] *Now it's for them that come after*'.[20]

With unemployment remaining just under three million until early 1933, there was a decline in union membership and dues. The TGWU leaders understood the need to push the message of social democracy to the mass of working people. They brought about the purchase of a newspaper, *The New Clarion* (influenced by Blatchford's original *Clarion*), and persuaded the TUC to invest in it. Bevin chaired the new company and the paper sold for 2d a copy at its launch on 11 June 1932. The weekly

19 Lovell and Roberts, *TUC*, p.131.
20 Published by Victor Gollancz and the TUC in 1934, p.96; emphasis added.

was to provide arguments and evidence for a progressive programme in everyday language. It failed after two years.

Issues associated with the wider economy and levels of employment spilled over into questions of race as well. Colonialism was backed by the TGWU leadership as strong supporters of Empire, but they were also aware of the hardships of black workers in the UK and in the colonies. According to most accounts, black workers, mainly from Africa and the West Indies with fewer from India and the Middle East, tended to live in the docklands of London, Liverpool, Cardiff, Bristol, and Glasgow. The numbers are estimated since there was no official record (the 1931 census was destroyed in a fire and the 1941 census was postponed). Best guesses are about 20,000 in total in the UK in the 1930s. Most were seafarers and their families, and there is an increasing number of accounts of their social and working lives.[21] Bevin exhibited ambiguous attitudes to colonial peoples and their rights. This hampered the TGWU solidarity with liberation movements, limited its ability to reconfigure economic policy away from imperial benefits, and created a disastrous lack of clarity in government policies towards the peoples of the Middle East, Southern Africa, the Indian subcontinent, and the West Indies. Much of this came to a head towards the end of the war.

In 1932 De Valera had assumed control in Ireland and this heralded further untangling of imperialist relations. Indian independence movements were stirring and the future relations with this 'jewel in the Crown' remained murky. Gandhi visited London and the workers in the Lancashire mills when in England in the autumn of 1931. India was the part of Empire that most concerned the TGWU leadership. John Cliff took note of the Royal Commission of Labour in India, and was especially interested in the docks (*The Record*, August and September 1931). Throughout the 1930s, Indian independence and the role of the trade unions was part of the TGWU's general policy towards Empire. Bevin spoke at the Labour Party conference in Southport in 1939, and while being proud of the Empire recognized the 'colonial problem' as one that needed urgent attention (*The Record*, July 1939). The coverage of Indian trade unionism was a mixture of support and somewhat patronizing efforts to offer a helping hand from those that know best.

In March 1935 the TUC adopted Circulars 16 and 17 ordering trades councils to ban delegates who were communists, communist associates, and fascists. The *Daily Worker* reported the outrage brought on by the conflation of fascism and communism (27 November 1934), and subsequent issuing of the so-called 'black circulars'.[22] Several union branches and

21 David Watson, 'Black Workers in London in the 1940s', *Historical Studies in Industrial Relations*, 1996, vol.1, no.1, pp.149–158.

22 K.G.J.C. Knowles, *Strikes: A Study in Industrial Conflict with Special Reference to British Experience Between 1911–1947* (Blackwell, 1952), pp.56–57.

trades councils were opposed to such a line.[23] Their position was clear:
'COMMUNISTS CANNOT BE CLASSED WITH FASCISTS [...]
We believe that to follow these suggestions will only result in splitting our
union activity [...] and prevent willing and capable members giving their
services to the union' (Daily Worker, 27 November 1934). Opposition to
capitalism from the left, especially from communists was anathema to
Citrine and Bevin. They backed the case against communist 'penetration'
and 'infiltration', because 'the Communist Party [...] set out to capture
positions of influence within individual trade unions'.[24]

Clashes with the communists remained the hallmark of the TGWU
under the Bevin supremacy.

> Not only did the communists seem to them no better than wreckers,
> but Communist propaganda appeared likely to terrify the middle
> class, at present quiescent, and drive it into supporting a Fascist
> movement in Britain [...] It seemed to be, therefore, essential both
> to bar the door to any Communist irruption, and to concentrate
> on moderate and 'gradualist' proposals.[25]

Trades councils in the 1930s were generally weak local organizations with hit-and-miss affiliations. They had been used to undermine
the NUWM's fight against unemployment, and '[d]oubtless, the elimina-
tion of the Trades Councils fitted in well with the growing movement
towards Trade Union centralisation. But it also made the Congress
less truly representative of rank-and-file opinion, and seriously
undermined the prestige of the Trades Councils as the local organs of
the movement'.[26]

In London, for example, '[t]he Council, as first and foremost an
organization of trade unionists, devoted a great part of this period to the
problem of unemployment'.[27] The Birmingham trades council also helped
the NUWM.[28] Such experiences were widespread and in Wolverhampton
the TC was subject to the same damaging policies from the TUC
in its 'unremitting hostility to the NUWCM [National Unemployed
Workers Committee Movement] combined with attempts to set up rival

---

23 Alan Clinton, *The Trade Union Rank and File: Trades Councils in Britain, 1900–40*
(Manchester University Press, 1977).
24 Allan Flanders, *Trade Unions* (Hutchinson, 1957), p.159.
25 Cole and Postgate, *Common People*, p.600.
26 Cole, *Trade Unionism*, p.192.
27 Julius Jacobs, *London Trades Council 1860–1950* (Lawrence & Wishart, 1950),
p.137.
28 John Corbett, *The Birmingham Trades Council 1855–1966* (Lawrence & Wishart,
1966), p.137.

organisations'.[29] The ban on communists was to be extended, if possible, to all union elected positions. In the autumn of 1935 reported opposition to such manoeuvres from within the TGWU came from members of the North-West London No 1/438 branch who urged Bevin to meet with them and explain his position.

At the 1935 Labour conference in Brighton, Lansbury maintained his pacifist stance and was brutally attacked by Bevin who won the day. 'It was Mr Ernest Bevin, the boss of the transport workers, massive and mastiff-like in appearance, shrewd and penetrating in intelligence, who put the picture into sharp perspective'.[30] As a result Labour was now committed to rearmament and the Party expressed the views of its members and supporters more truly.

The general election on 14 November 1935 was a resounding victory for the Conservatives now led by Stanley Baldwin. Labour, under Clement Attlee, made large net gains of over a hundred seats. It was a muddle of epic proportions on all sides, and with a very low turnout the only surprise was the election of the communist MP for West Fife, William Gallacher. He was the only MP consistently and unwaveringly to oppose Hitler. The vote was a clear mandate for rearmament and when Hitler invaded the Rhineland on 7 March 1936, the British government started to accelerate the process.

At the 1935 conference in Douglas on the Isle of Man, the left opposition, mainly through the Rank-and-File Committee, sought to hold Bevin and Deakin to account. They knew the majority of delegates would back the leadership, but the point was to make the case, open the debate, and post notice of intent. Some of the anger was directed at the union's own democratic systems and protocols – power of officials, election of officers, and the EC's powers to call strikes. Bevin was defeated on the issue of raising subs. He wanted more money to expand into road haulage and the car factories, but the delegates refused.

Unemployment, and the Unemployed Workers' Struggles

Unemployment was the crippling heart of British economic life and working-class struggles. Its importance for TGWU members and the union as a whole was clear: it undermined bargaining and thus put pressure on wages and conditions; it split the movement with communists fighting for betterment now rather than passively waiting for the next

29 George Barnsby, *A History of Wolverhampton, Bilston, & District Trades Union Council 1865–1990* (Wolverhampton Trades Council, 1994), p.52.
30 'CATO', *Guilty Men* (Victor Gollancz, 1943), p.32.

Labour government to save them; and it fostered a generation of reformers in favour of state intervention to maintain full employment.

As *The Times* was later to claim: 'Next to war, unemployment has been the most widespread, the most insidious, and the most corroding malady of our generation' (23 January 1943). Despite the slump technically lasting until late in 1933, there was growth to go with decline and new industrial sectors to match the old dying ones. In other words capitalism was responding, as it had always done, to the trade/business cycles and Kondratieff long waves (forty- to sixty-year cycles of high and low economic growth), by ruining the lives of millions of workers while at the same time lifting others up into new jobs with new skills in new and expanding enterprises. With the peak of unemployment in early 1933 (at about three million) there were signs of partial recovery based on the devaluation of the pound, cheap money, and the controversial use of tariffs with imperial preference, lower tariffs on trade between countries of the Empire. These developments were reflected in the membership of the TGWU which fell from 408,374 in 1931 to 372,992 by 1932 (a drop of 8.7 per cent). This represented a loss of income, influence, and reputation. With the end of the recession and the growth of new industrial sectors open to TGWU recruitment, the union had 493,266 members by 1935, and by 1937 it was the largest in the country.

Both the slump and the recovery were uneven across sectors and regions. It was formed on a producer-dominated control of supply with iron, steel, and coal production on the rise, agriculture subsidized by the state, and cotton and shipbuilding falling away. With stable wages and falling prices more and more workers and their families decided to spend. It was this, as Keynes later codified,[31] that lifted the nation out of the slump. There was a huge rise in the use of electricity at home and, therefore, the demand for electrical appliances (vacuum cleaners, refrigerators, sewing machines); as well as for cars, plastics and nylon, and housing, especially during the start of the slum clearances after 1934. The subsequent building boom and start of rearmament reduced unemployment.

The Great Crash of 1929 and subsequent slump meant that, 'for those who, by definition, had no control over or access to the means of production [...] [n]amely, men and women hired for wages, the primary consequence of the slump was unemployment on an unimagined and unprecedented scale, and for longer than anyone had ever expected'. In the worst years 1932–1933 about 22 per cent of the British labour force were out of work. Even with the recovery after 1933, average unemployment for the decade remained at about 17 per cent. 'What made it even more dramatic was that public provision for social security, including

---

31 J.M. Keynes, *The General Theory of Employment, Interest and Money* (MacMillan, 1936).

unemployment relief, was either non-existent, as in the USA, or [...] extremely meagre, especially for the long-term unemployed'. Economic security was always a vital concern of working people – fear of the lack of protection from sickness, accidents at work, and old age was a driving force behind their politics and way of life. In the 1930s only about 60 per cent of people were covered by any form of such insurance. 'Hence the central, the traumatic, impact of mass unemployment on the politics of the industrialised countries'. Despite the fact that many workers were better off due to falling prices, especially food prices, throughout the 1930s, nonetheless, 'the image which dominated at the time was that of soup kitchens, of unemployed "Hunger Marchers" from smokeless settlements where no steel or ships were made converging on capital cities to denounce those they held responsible'.[32]

At the time traditional economists dismissed the depression years as an aberration of the system, but others saw it 'not as the Great Exception but as the normal outcome of the workings of the American economic system'.[33] This argument is central to the thinking of the leaders of the TGWU as they expressed their task as softening the blows meted out to the working classes by recessions, and clinging to the wishfulness that such recessions could be abolished. As part of that, attacking the left of the political spectrum, associated with militancy inside the union, was seen as not rocking the boat of reformed capitalism and not upsetting the social order by fermenting revolution.

Critically for TGWU members, those in work also had tough times with, for example, wage cuts among Lancashire and Cheshire water workers, and Scottish Motor Traction Company; lay-offs in the building trades; the adverse impact of the sliding scale among quarrymen; and industrial diseases such as silicosis among pottery workers.

It was this 'industrial reserve army' and the wider failed economic policies and nostrums that not only enabled employers to cut wages but empowered union leaders, such as Bevin, to negotiate wage cuts. The defenders of such policies argue that it was better to accept a wage cut than a job loss, and that it was better still to negotiate cuts than have them imposed by the employers. The TGWU GEC took that view, especially as it enabled the union to keep its seat around the bargaining table and thereby preserve the integrity of its position and hold onto its members.

The NUWM was the main vehicle through which the demands of the unemployed and their families were made.[34] It met with hostility from Conservatives, and by many union leaders, including those at the TGWU,

32 All quotes in this paragraph are from Hobsbawm, *Age of Extremes*, pp.92–93.
33 Paul Baran and Paul Sweezy, *Monopoly Capital: An Essay on the American Economic and Social Order* (Pelican, 1966), p.235.
34 Roger Seifert, 'Wal Hannington and the Unemployed Workers' Struggles in Britain in the 1930s', *Theory and Struggle*, 2021, vol.122, no.1, pp.8–21; Ralph

who saw it as a communist-led rebellion likely to undermine their negotiations and their political position. As one trenchant critic explained: 'The unions' inability to cope with unemployment was not merely rooted in their conceptions of themselves as bargainers with employers. Political considerations obtruded as well'. As a result the leaders of the TGWU stood aloof from the need to have a grass roots organization of the unemployed. 'The consequence was that throughout the interwar years the Communist Party, bitterly vilified as it was, provided (in alliance with other left-wingers) the only strenuous opposition to unemployment'.[35]

The majority of registered unemployed were manual workers in stable industries of textiles, steel, shipbuilding, and coal mining. Hence the uneven geographical spread with South Wales, Scotland, and the North East hardest hit. The subsequent ill health and social deprivation that came with starvation was stark for all those willing to see. And 'it was women who faced the intensification of domestic labour and grinding poverty associated with unemployment'.[36] The Anomalies Regulations of 1931, which restricted rights to unemployment insurance, meant that most married women were taken off the register and were refused unemployment benefit.[37] In the early 1930s the unemployed were subject to terrible iniquities born from the means test, used to determine if people had the means by which to support themselves rather than receive government benefits. The British Medical Association (BMA) reported that the payments were inadequate to feed people, and it was destroying the family unit.[38]

It was in the slum areas that the passionate desire for welfare was developed, as self-help community groups, along with local left political activists and some trade unionists, turned the tide that helped to create the welfare state. It was the women and men of the 'depressed areas' fighting for every scrap of dignity and hope that created the popular sentiment that became the national mood for reform.

In the 1930s the NUWM organized a series of hunger marches, a tradition going back to the Blanketeers.[39] The September 1932 hunger march, for example, started in Scotland, with 1,500 converging on

Hayburn, 'The National Unemployed Workers' Movement, 1921–36', *International Review of Social History*, 1983, vol.28, no.3, pp.279–295.

35 Tony Lane, *The Union Makes Us Strong* (Arrow Books, 1974), p.132.

36 Richard Croucher, *We Refuse to Starve in Silence: A History of the National Unemployed Workers' Movement, 1920–1946* (Lawrence & Wishart, 1987), p.17.

37 Branson and Heinemann, *Britain in the 1930s*, p.32.

38 Barry K. Hill, 'Women and Unemployment in Birmingham 1918–1939', *Midland History*, 2002, vol.27, no.1, pp.130–145.

39 The Blanketeers or Blanket March was a demonstration organised in Manchester in March 1817. The intention was for the participants, who were mainly Lancashire weavers, to march to London.

Figure 1: NUWM 1934 march in Plymouth
Credit: From *Daily Worker* archive at Marx Memorial Library

London. One leading trade unionist recalls: 'I took part in a march from South Wales to Bristol, as an unemployed man, urging the trade unions to take more positive action against the means test for work or full mainte-nance for the unemployed. We had a pretty rough reception both by the police and the Trade Union Congress'. He was arrested and noted that 'the deputation that tried to get into the Congress Hall to put the case was ejected, and Wal Hannington [...] was thrown down the steps'.[40]

In February 1933 the NUWM claimed over 100,000 members in 349 branches, 36 district councils, and 34 women's sections. It played a major role in formulating policy and forcing the unions and Labour to take up more radical economic and social programmes. The triumph of the movement was seen in forcing the hand of the government to grant more support for the unemployed alongside a national debate (in which the NUWM was excluded) through the BBC on forms of non-monetary amelioration. The TUC and the TGWU sought to undermine the NUWM with alternative organizational schemes for the unemployed through trades councils.

40 Will Paynter, *British Trade Unions and the Problem of Change* (George Allen & Unwin, 1970), pp.22–23.

At the 1935 TUC the TGWU delegates attacked the NUWM, and with Bevin's blessing, opposed any links with NUWM and Wal Hannington. At the time the TUC issued the so-called 'black circulars' seeking to ban communists from union office, and Bevin himself spoke of the need to 'refuse credentials to persons who might be members of either Fascist or Communist organisations' in order to defeat the communists and 'the most nefarious practices that this movement has ever had to face' (*The Record*, September 1935).

Hannington wrote a class-based study of unemployment which is crystal clear about the evidence, the events, and the causes of both unemployment and the subsequent hardships.[41] He is particularly angry at the fate of younger workers, the use of effective 'slave camps', and the danger that the siren xenophobic voices of British fascists might persuade some of the unemployed to seek dangerous liaisons. Unemployment 'has been a matter of grave concern not only to vast numbers of the population who have themselves experienced unemployment, but also to those who have been fortunate enough to escape it, yet have been constantly haunted by the fear that at any moment it may draw them into its vortex'.[42] This grasp of class politics and appreciation of the central role of class struggle meant that the hunger marches, the agitations and demonstrations, and the organization of the NUWM itself reflected the realities of class power and the balance of class forces. Such a position served the movement well, and it was that more than anything else that frightened and disturbed the TGWU leaders.

The final clause of the NUWM constitution reads 'that our movement shall keep before itself the ultimate goal of working-class power'.[43] The NUWM forced a change of direction by the government: 'This is what mass action has been able to do [...] [I]t is an emphatic answer to those tame reformist Labour leaders who have consistently told the workers that they must wait till the next General Election before they can remedy their grievances'.[44] As a result of the consciousness raising activities of the NUWM state policymakers were shifting their ground as witnessed in the 1944 White Paper which stated: 'The Government accept as one of its primary aims and responsibilities the maintenance of a high and stable level of employment after the war'.[45]

Collective bargaining in a cold climate for TGWU members made ending unemployment more important. Despite some recovery by the end of 1933, mass unemployment in the old industrial areas clouded the

41 Wal Hannington, *Unemployed Struggles, 1919–1936: My Life and Struggles Amongst the Unemployed* (EP Publishing, 1936), p.13.
42 Wal Hannington, *Ten Lean Years* (Victor Gollancz, 1940), p.7.
43 Noreen Branson, *History of the Communist Party of Great Britain, 1927–1941* (Lawrence & Wishart, 1985), p.75.
44 Branson, *Communist Party*, p.82.
45 HMSO, *Employment Policy* (May 1944, Cmd. 6527), p.3.

picture. *Love on the Dole* by Walter Greenwood captured the bitter nature of such living, but the devastation was there for all to see.[46] The TGWU focused on supply-side solutions inside the labour market and its flows with alternative economic policies routed in state planning. The failures of the current system were in plain sight: 'the so-called National Government have failed, as we said they would [...] [capitalism] has caused over production, falling prices, collapse of trade, large-scale unemployment, and millions of workers find themselves in the critical position of having to starve in the midst of abundance' (*The Record*, January 1933). The solution was to fight for the new 'social order' and vote Labour.

Meanwhile the duality of the UK labour market was maintained with growth in large factories in the Midlands and the south, and by the unrelenting unemployment of declining industrial sectors. Bevin understood the need to solve the question for two reasons: his unremitting hatred of poverty and the notion of men and women being forced into idleness; and the recognition that long-term unemployment alongside the much-hated means test were no advert for his brand of worker-facing capitalism. In his pamphlet 'My plan for 2,000,000 workers' (based on articles in *The New Clarion* in 1933) he argued for incentives to retire early for those over 60 and for those disabled by wounds or sickness; an increase in the school leaving age to 16; and the start of a 40-hour week. This entirely supply-side inspired solution to remove the equivalent of two million jobs from the labour market showed the limitations of Bevin's desire for change.

In March and April 1934 Bevin wrote two articles for *The Record* in which he recognized that the ideological grip of laissez-faire economic policy was loosening in favour of more and more targeted state intervention. At both the 1934 TUC and Labour Party conferences, the TGWU tabled motions to protect industries and to urge local government to step in where central government had failed.

A key campaign for the TGWU was the shorter working week. The aim was for a basic 40-hours based on a five-day week. A point taken up again by Bevin in the autumn of 1936 as reported in the *Daily Worker*:

Mr. Ernest Bevin [...] moved that 'The effect of a well-planned working week would be to flatten out production over the year [...] In many industries it is already being accomplished and much of the seasonal fluctuations can be avoided[...] After all, the five-day working week is not the millennium. Old Moses gave us six days about 5,000 years ago, and that was for a nomadic population. Surely, after 5,000 years modern science can give us one more day's rest in seven?'

46 Walter Greenwood, *Love on the Dole* (Jonathan Cape, 1933). The novel was made into a play in 1934 and into a film in 1941.

Mondism and the Official Collective Bargaining Strategy of the TGWU

A critical lens through which to understand the labour movement's trials and tribulations in the 1930s is that of Mondism. It dominated TGWU policy in these years. Essentially, this outlook rejected any opposition to developments within modern capitalism, and sold partnership with capital to the workers in the name of increased efficiency of production. The central case was that through co-operation there would be productivity gains and these would be shared with the workers in terms of higher wages and better conditions. In this mould rationalization of capital was seen as an efficient speed-up rather than as a means to greater exploitation. This was 'Taylorism', a pseudo-scientific form of time and motion study, with a trade union face, and that meant opposition to any struggles against compromise and partnership.

The ideal solution pushed by the TGWU was that union officials would negotiate in partnership with the employers and thus bring about an 'equitable share in the gains resulting from increased productivity'.[47] Citrine gave a series of lectures to the 1929 TUC summer school which emphasized the direction of the British economy as being towards centralization and concentration of ownership. After 1918, union amalgamations made it easier to organize the TUC, and it was 'headed from 1926 onwards, by an energetic and enterprising General Secretary, Walter Citrine, determined to make the TUC a power in the land', and 'the radically changed conception of trade unionism as a willing and essential partner in the conduct of the nation's economic affairs steadily gained acceptance'.[48] Indeed, the TGWU set about seeking national negotiations for tramways, dockers, rubber workers, and in flour milling. These sometimes worked, especially after 1934 with the tighter labour market, but frequently failed to deliver.

The TGWU fully supported the drive to make industry more prosperous and more efficient, and by 1944 a TUC report on post-war reconstruction strongly favoured nationalization as a means to greater efficiency and therefore greater prosperity for the working class as a whole. The TGWU became more strident in its calls for public ownership, and at the 1933 BDC it called for 'public ownership and workers' control' of industry (*The Record*, August 1933).

Bevin used his union's power to shift the balance inside the TUC away from miners and textile workers and more towards the newer sectors of transport, manufacturing, and building. 'The new attitude of the unions made possible the Mond-Turner discussions of 1927–9,

47 Allen Hutt, *British Trade Unionism: A Short History* (Lawrence & Wishart, 1975), p.120.
48 Flanders, *Trade Unions*, pp.21–22.

in which members of the General Council of the TUC and a group of influential employers considered the establishment of Citrine's proposed institutions of industrial co-operation'.[49] Bevin represented the majority of sentiment inside the TGWU when he eschewed strikes, and argued that 'reason' was a better ally for his members than action.[50] This acceptance of the ideological and practical issues behind Mondism stayed with the TGWU leadership throughout the 1930s and beyond.[51]

Their position was that capitalism provided jobs and that unions should help capitalists be more efficient and productive as this would allow for ever-increasing standards of living as long as the unions could bargain, be heard, and be taken seriously. Hence their accommodation with 'speed-up' and their willingness to share joint bodies with employers. This was predicated on the achievements from years of union struggles, because 'in well-organized industries the power of arbitrary dismissal, the very centre of its [capitalism] authority, is being shaken'.[52] It was this fundamental that Bevin applied with great vigour to the strategic bargaining position of the TGWU.

Bevin persuasively argued that the task of trade unionism through collective bargaining was to adjust terms and conditions to the efficiency and profitability of the firm through recognized machinery backed by government. In essence the TGWU leadership took the view, repeated through the Donovan Commission in the late 1960s, that formal procedures set up for collective bargaining purposes were the way forward in terms of representation and recognition. In this manner the union could be built larger and stronger, the members could see their interests being defended, and employers, including the state, had to make terms. In particular he pleaded with members to pay their subs (*The Record*, March 1935) and he endlessly damned the problem of non-unionization (*The Record*, January 1935). This would meet Bevin's political aims as well, as such systems were partly designed to sideline the syndicalist tendencies among sections of the TGWU membership, alongside communists and other militants. Collective bargaining is by its nature a method to avoid open conflict and to moderate both wage cuts and wage increases.

The employers and their political backers knew this, and sought at every opportunity to weaken collective resolve, struggles, and class identity. The ability to divide and rule was partly rooted in fear of job loss, and partly it succeeded because religious, social, and political leaders pushed their own narrow identity agendas. In many ways this came

49 Hugh Clegg and T.E. Chester, 'Joint Consultation', in Allan Flanders and Hugh Clegg, *The System of Industrial Relations in Great Britain* (Blackwell, 1967), p.336.
50 Ben Roberts, *National Wages Policy in War and Peace* (George Allen & Unwin, 1958).
51 Allen, *Trade Union Leadership*, p.103.
52 R.H. Tawney, *The Acquisitive Society* (G. Bell and Sons, 1926), p.175.

down to a Manichaean battle between those who supported capitalist employers as wealth creators and job providers, and who therefore sought accommodation with them through partnership, concession bargaining, and sweetheart deals. These proponents could honestly and with justification argue for better pay and conditions, they could fight for fairer outcomes, they could build strong unions and collective bargaining machinery, they could back strikes in some circumstances, and be presented as hard-headed realists. They rejected a clash of class interests, opposed class struggle, and set about destroying those who preached such subversion. They accepted knighthoods, damehoods, and peerages. They sat on government committees, on boards, and fought for a 'moderate' leadership of the Labour Party. They were not only the architects of Mondism, but were true believers in its efficacy.

On the other side was arrayed the serried ranks of leftist thinkers and activists. They were the proponents of both the United Front and Popular Front against fascism at home and abroad, they backed the NUWM, they fought for the Spanish Republic and against Italian annexation of Abyssinia, and they understood the nature of class struggle. The struggle was over wages and conditions, job security, against speed-up and exploitation, for fair rents, just benefits, proper pensions, good health and education, and equal opportunities for all.

As TGWU member Emile Burns explains, the theory and practice of right-wing labour depends on constantly redefining both capitalism and socialism in ways that allow them to pose as anti-capitalist and pro-socialist, since large numbers of labour voters are workers desperate for a new beginning. In the 1930s Bevin and his allies in the trade union movement and Attlee as the Labour leader (after October 1935) could argue that they were anti-capitalist socialists, because the old form of exploitative capitalism was on the way out partly due to joint bargaining arrangements with trade unions. They argued that their form of socialism could be achieved by keeping private profit and major corporations but bending them to the will of a reforming Labour government.[53] In addition the TGWU affiliated over 300,000 members to the Labour Party and so Mondism went political.

The main hotspot with regard to unofficial strike action in the TGWU was the London busmen, but there were also several wildcat stoppages in confrontation with management over 'speed-up' in factories, hiring and firing on the waterfront, hours in transport, and over-pay on Dublin trams. A prime factor in the propensity to strike has always been the efficacy of control over the short-term supply of labour to the employer – the workers' power derived from the refusal to work. The main issues can be reduced to developments in trade unionism itself concerning the composition of the membership and the question of control over strikes and strike funds by national union executives. The centralizing tendency of which the TGWU was a major example meant it was harder to call strikes without official sanction, and the London busmen's rank and file had its officials suspended after the 1937 dispute.[54]

While the main coverage in such bargaining remained all the issues associated with pay and payment systems, and a wide range of conditions including hours of work, there were also increasingly important matters of health and safety. As new industries expanded they brought with them new work-related illnesses and dangers, and with that came employer denial and union fight. The busmen, for example, suffered from stomach complaints due to long hours sitting down and with very short meal breaks.[55] Work-based diseases and accidents created pressure to regulate and compensate such victims of careless employers – careless with their workers' lives. This theme of prevention of industrial accidents and disease loomed large as did the need for proper compensation. The latter was taken up at the 1933 BDC (*The Record*, August 1933), as were, more generally, speed limits among the Road Transport Passenger (RTP) and Road Transport Commercial (RTC) groups, gangway dangers in the docks and waterways (the safety charter for dockers was launched in 1932), and dust and dirt in flour milling and tinplate working. The TGWU fought hard for better health and safety, and more compensation (*The Record*, August 1937).

The 'Frontier of Control' and Local Strikes

Corporations have neither bodies to be punished, nor souls to be condemned; they therefore do as they like.[56]

The propertyless working class emerged as a common category in the industrial era (after the end of slavery and serfdom). In and of themselves, they cannot earn a wage to feed their families (the British MI5's maxim is that society is 'four meals away from anarchy') because they neither own land for rent nor capital for profits. They own their ability to labour – that is what they sell, their labour power, for wages as income in a commodified labour market.[57]

There is, therefore, a clash of interests between employers and employees fought out in various ways, and reflected in different tactics

---

54 Knowles, *Strikes*, p.23.

55 Rhodri Hayward, 'Busman's Stomach and the Embodiment of Modernity', *Contemporary British History*, 2017, vol.31, no.1, pp.1–23.

56 Attributed to Edward Thurlow, Lord Chancellor of Great Britain 1778–1792.

57 Edward Thompson, *The Making of the English Working Class* (Penguin, 1963).

as exemplified by official and unofficial organization and action. At the workplace the imagery of trench warfare remained strong, and when used to conjure up such a conflict at work between workers and bosses, it resonated with the workforce.[58] This allows for both formal disputes over job regulation,[59] and action seen as part of a wider class struggle.[60] 'Strikes in the broad sense – collective stoppages of work undertaken in order to bring pressure to bear on those who depend on the sale or use of the products of that work – are almost as old as work itself'.[61] The right to strike is guarded by workers since it is their main weapon against the power imbalance with employers. Therefore, to abandon the use of strikes, either through bargaining compromises or state legislation, can be seen as a weakening of the collective power of workers. Unofficial strikes (ones not sanctioned by union rules) and unconstitutional strikes (ones in breach of agreed procedures) reflect a widespread awareness that the exercise of worker power at the place of work trumps any niceties of union and bargaining regulations. In the 1930s and 1940s these were certainly part of the armoury of rank-and-file members in the TGWU, especially with the reluctance of TGWU leadership to support action.

The idea of a 'general strike' or even large-scale sympathy strikes in support of one group have always had a tinge of revolution about them, but by the 1930s both official strikes and general strikes were muted by recession and recent history. While strikes are clear cut, a range of options (action short of a strike) are available from go-slows and work-to-rules to overtime bans, and withdrawal of goodwill. The level of violence from sabotage to fighting on picket lines, and the involvement of police (and sometimes secret police) were an ever present aspect of strikes throughout these years.

With the growth of the modern corporation came the growth in what was then modern management methods – McKinsey's management consultancy, for example, was founded in 1926 and began to influence UK firms' behaviour by the late 1930s. The decade saw the start of a more 'professional' approach to management of labour. Shop-floor workers resented and opposed the imposition of new measures, but most accepted them in exchange for a bargain that included job security, better wages, and improved conditions. As factories grew so their owners grew into large corporations, driven by USA examples, and rooted in a clearer focus on profitability. These joint stock companies brought pressure to bear on both governments and unions. It was this that persuaded the

58 Carter Goodrich, *The Frontier of Control: A Study in British Workshop Politics* (Harcourt, Brace and Howe, 1920).
59 Hugh Clegg, *The System of Industrial Relations in Great Britain* (Blackwell, 1970).
60 Richard Hyman, *Industrial Relations: A Marxist Introduction* (MacMillan, 1975).
61 Knowles, *Strikes*, p.1.

TGWU that doing deals, coming to terms, with large employers with their inward investment schemes, would consolidate union organization, provide stability in employment, and allow union influence to grow.

There was a shift in employment with the decline in mining and textiles, and the rise in engineering and chemicals. Between 1932 and 1945, for example, the number of males working in engineering, shipbuilding and metal trades rose from 1,521,000 to 2,373,000 and the number of females in that sector rose from 281,000 to 1,109,000.

The applications of modern labour management in those factories and workshops were sloganized under the term 'Taylorism', named after F.W. Taylor and his scientific management revolution.[62] Taylorism has been with us ever since. Marxists' analysis of the labour process was part of the case against the intensification of exploitation through degrading work.[63] The tension between internal labour markets and occupational labour markets in terms of the utilization of skills matters because it fed directly into both trade union and government policy.[64]

As factories grew in size, so wage systems such as Payments By Results meant that plant-based stewards could bargain without official support. This trend forced Bevin to adopt an ever-increasing officer-led bargaining strategy linking JICs with plant-level agreements. These were backed by tight procedural regulations as at Rover in Coventry, Longbridge in Birmingham, and Mander in Wolverhampton. There were outbreaks of strike action in 1933, for example, at Venesta Plywood in East London, Ford at Dagenham, and Firestone tyres in Brentford. Another typical case was among tramway staff in 1934 in Bradford when the employers sought to cut and run from the national agreement. Despite TGWU officials' weak handling of the matter, the workers voted at a midnight meeting of over 800 to fight for the national scheme.

TGWU leaders sought to dampen down the rising wave of militancy among its own members because, 'recovery did not bring with it a softening of class antagonisms. Rather there was a more aggressive tone of class war'.[65] One key issue was the extent to which the industrial sector was sheltered from or exposed to foreign competition. In building trades and railways, for example, the trend towards 'a highly-centralized and complete system of national joint regulation of wages and working conditions continued unbroken'.[66]

---

62 F.W. Taylor, *The Principles of Scientific Management* (Harper and Brothers, 1919).
63 Harry Braverman, *Labor and Monopoly Capitalism: The Degradation of Work in the Twentieth Century* (Monthly Review Press, 1974).
64 Charles More, 'Reskilling and Labour Markets in Britain c.1890–1940: Questions and Hypotheses', 1996, *Historical Studies in Industrial Relations*, vol.2, no.1, pp.93–110.
65 Taylor, *English History*, p.346.
66 Allan Flanders, 'Collective Bargaining' in Flanders and Clegg, *Industrial Relations*, p.279.

Other sectors had accepted Whitley-style JIC systems, but, for example, for wool and textiles it collapsed under the strain from imports.[67] The main success stories for collective bargaining through JICs were public administration, public utilities (gas, water, electric), and transport other than railways and road haulage. Where there was a strong combine of employers, they kept to the voluntary system as with, for example, bricks, cement, flour milling, and chemicals.[68] The TGWU was the main proponent of JICs among trade unions.

The strike record of this period is often characterized as limp with little regard for the thousands of unreported disputes across the land. TGWU members were involved in disputes in the docks, on the buses, and in manufacturing. The total number of recorded strikes fluctuated, but was 389 in 1932 rising dramatically to 1,129 by 1937, and then again to 2,293 by 1945. While the majority remained in coal mining, there was a sharp increase in the engineering and metal trades from 46 to 612 at its peak in 1943.

In 1936 Charlie Chaplin's film, *Modern Times*, was shown in British cinemas. It depicts a factory worker having to tighten nuts as they pass him on a conveyor belt. The management introduce more speed-up including a machine to feed him thereby abolishing lunch breaks. It was a silent movie because Chaplin believed that the message would reach more audiences and represent a greater sense of alienation and powerlessness at work. This portrayal of factory work as the modern malaise of alienation was reflected elsewhere in the works on the justice system (Kafka's *The Trial*, 1937), and captured in the bitter absurdism of Evelyn Waugh's *A Handful of Dust* (1934), and JRR Tolkien's light-versus-darkness story *The Hobbit* (1937).

One major example of this lampooned movement was the eponymously named Bedaux system.[69] In 1933 the TUC produced a 2d pamphlet. In its foreword Citrine wrote: 'many industrial disputes have been caused by reason of its introduction, and in almost every case where the system is operated, the workers view it with the deepest suspicion and resentment', and 'only where the workers are strongly organised in a Trade Union can they hope to avoid excessive speeding-up'.[70] The study found that '[t]he Bedaux System is only one of a large number of systems of payment by results [...] for ensuring an additional wage payment for output in excess of a given standard'.[71]

The engineer installing the system carries out a time and motion study and then creates a measure of time and pay associated with some rate or

67 Whitley councils were established in 1919 as an example of state-sponsored JICs.
68 Flanders, 'Collective Bargaining', p.282.
69 Charles Bedaux, 'Overcoming Time Study Fear', *Personnel Journal*, 1935, vol.8, no.6, pp.335–337.
70 *The TUC Examines the Bedaux System of Payment by Results* (TUC, 1933), p.1.
71 TUC, *Bedaux*, p.4.

standard. The TUC report concludes: 'any method of unlimited speeding-up and overdriving is opposed to the whole spirit of Trade Unionism. No support can be given to any method which reduces the workers to the status of machines'.[72]

In practice most opposition came from the shop floor. In 1932 Bedaux claimed that 50,000 workers in 32 factories were under the system, and by 1936 (*Labour Research*, June 1936) there were 240 firms involved. 'Towards the end of the depression and at the beginning of the rearmament boom, when the Bedaux system was being introduced into a number of factories, there was an increase in militancy which was more favourable to Communist agitation', as with strikes at Lucas in Birmingham, Firestone, Ford in London, and Pressed Steel at Cowley.[73]

This anti-Bedaux series of unofficial strikes,[74] included one at Richard Johnson and Nephew in Manchester in 1934. A report in *The Times* quoted the renowned socialist barrister, D.N. Pritt: 'The Bedaux experts had beset the workmen by standing over them with note-books and stop-watches, as it were, breathing down their necks while they were doing their difficult and responsible work'.[75] In the autumn of 1930 there was a strike at the Rover factory over the dismissal of eight women for refusing to work under Bedaux. The company decided to bring in Bedaux through what they perceived to be the weakest group of workers – non-unionized women. The 150 women involved rejected the proposal outright, because '[t]he women saw no reason to abandon the current piecework system'.[76]

> The conflict at Rover gave the T & G the first of several opportunities to gain a foothold in Coventry's engineering shops [...] But enrolling in the T & G did not solve the women's problems; far from it. Though ready to fight tooth and nail against an unreconstructed Bedauxism, the T & G leadership had long been enchanted by the prospect of joint participation in the project to revive industry through rationalization.[77]

72 TUC, *Bedaux*, p.16.
73 Claude Berridge (May 1933), 'The Ford Strikers Win a Victory', *Labour Monthly*; Sam Shelton (February 1934), 'Strike Struggles in Birmingham', *Labour Monthly*; E. Woolley (June 1934), 'The May Day Strike at Lucas', *Labour Monthly*.
74 Kevin Whitston, 'Worker Resistance and Taylorism in Britain', *International Review of Social History*, 1997, vol.42, no.1, pp.1–24.
75 Cited in Mick Jenkins, *Time & Motion Strike, Manchester 1934–7: The Wiredrawers' Struggle Against the Bedaux System at Richard Johnson's* (Our History pamphlet, 1974).
76 Laura Lee Downs, 'Industrial Decline, Rationalization and Equal Pay: The Bedaux Strike at Rover Automobile Company', *Social History*, 1990, vol.15, no.1, pp.45–73, p.61.
77 Downs, 'Industrial Decline', p.62.

The TGWU's official, Andrew Dalgleish, opposed the introduction of Bedaux, but he was willing to compromise.

> Dalgleish and the eight others deputed to investigate the scheme met with the Bedaux consultants and toured two engineering firms where the system was already being worked [...] Dalgleish and the other T & G people appear to have convinced themselves that, with certain crucial amendments, Bedauxism might be interpreted as conforming to the 'customs and agreements'.[78]

The TGWU did recognize the strike and sent Alice Arnold to organize the members. They formed picket lines to stop strike breakers despite harassment from local police. The importance of their 20-day strike meant that Bevin himself negotiated a settlement with the Rover management. The deal was finally accepted in which the women received higher pay for faster more intensive work. This trade off was fraught since the TGWU opposed Bedaux in principle but fudged the issue if it meant higher wages – the core of the union's approach to modern management, namely that the union should, indeed had a duty, to negotiate speed-up and higher productivity with safeguards and some extra rewards. In June 1932 *The Record* reported that Rover had abandoned Bedaux.

Events at the Lucas factory in Birmingham provide further insight into the struggles involved in 'speed-up'. The harsh reality on the factory floor showed both the methods and the outcomes of such developments to be far from the idealized hopes of the official TGWU negotiators. The factory was big, and it was this level of capital concentration that brought together a huge army of labour, especially women with a strong sense of common identity. In January 1931 Jessie Eden noticed someone standing behind her and asked what was going on. 'They said they were timing me... the fact was that I'd always worked quickly... they obviously wanted to set the time by me and the others would have to keep up with it'.[79] A rank-and-file committee of 40, representing ten shops, was set up. Jesse Eden went to the TGWU officials, she said, 'they looked at me amazed when I brought the application forms filled up'. Most of the women joined the TGWU then and there.

The new Bedaux payments system claimed to scientifically measure the natural unit of production in one minute, and rewards were offered for accomplishing more than 60 units in an hour. Oliver Lucas had visited the USA and became a convert of the system. Nonetheless, 140 women refused to carry on co-operating with the project. Faced with a complete stoppage of work, a notice was issued by Lucas discontinuing

---

78 Downs, 'Industrial Decline', p.63.
79 Graham Stevenson, *The Real Jessie Eden* (Our History, 2020).

the system. The effects of the Lucas strike rumbled on in other local factories, for example, *The Hand Weight* was the bulletin of the rank-and-file committee of the scale makers at Hope's works in Smethwick where 3,500 workers challenged the introduction of the Bedaux system. Three years later there was another strike by Lucas workers to stop the use of speed-up, and this was typical of disputes across the new factories in the Midlands.

Another important strike involving TGWU members at factory level was at Pressed Steel in Oxford. The strike started on Friday 13 July 1934 (*The Record*, July 1934). Employees on the night shift in the press shop were paid short on their wages. They stopped work and elected a deputation, consisting of four women and 12 men, to meet management the next morning. They declared their work as 'slave conditions' for 'pin-money', since their wages were consistently lower than men's for an identical job.

The deputation was turned down. The following Monday, 100 night shift workers walked out and the deputation became a provisional strike committee. Local communists advised the strike committee to include demands for higher pay, better conditions, and trades' union recognition. The CP sent Abe Lazarus, a leading communist organizer, to Oxford to support the local branch.[80] He came along with two full-time organizers from the TGWU and shortly after his arrival Lazarus was made chair of the strike committee. On the same day 180 workers in the press shop walked out. The message to the manager simply stated that the strikers would not go back to work until better wages were agreed.

On the first day the managing director refused to see a deputation hurriedly got together to present the strikers' case. The *Oxford Mail* reported that the number out had increased to 600. The same day a second mass meeting was held and officers from the TGWU addressed the strikers. Some provisional demands were submitted to management. A special bulletin, *The Conveyer*, was issued by the local TGWU. It stated that 'the whole of the working class in Oxford is stirred by the magnificent stand of the strikers'.

On Monday 23rd, the strike committee met with management for the first time. Otto Müeller, the managing director, issued a statement with no reference to wages and conditions and a refused to recognize the union. The strikers rejected this out of hand. The strike had gained support within the local community, and workers in Dagenham, Coventry, and Birmingham refused to handle goods from the factory. By 24 July the strikers were still determined to continue the fight for the abolition of all piecework; 18s 6d; flat-rate bonus for all departments; no victimization; and 100 per cent trade unionism. On 28 July the strike had been

80   Geoff Andrews, 'Abe Lazarus and the Lost World of British Communism', *History Workshop Journal*, 2017, vol.83, no.1, pp.272–288.

won,[81] even though 'the TGWU regional officer for the Midlands roundly condemned the unofficial strikes at Pressed Steel'.[82] The strikers returned to work with a guaranteed basic hourly rate, no victimization, and full union recognition. 1,500 workers joined unions at the factory. The national union leadership was worried by the strength of the communists among TGWU activists, because '[w]hen the Pressed Steel Company was forced to recognise the trade unions in 1934, this was the result of some vigorous local activity with communist party support'.[83]

Two other strikes involving women and the TGWU captured the mood. In the summer of 1934 there was a strike by the 'Mullard girls' in Mitcham over pay parity with the factory in Balham (*The Record*, July 1934). The TGWU officials were unhelpful to the strikers working in a radio valve factory. A deputation of strikers went to the TGWU offices to demand that any return to work was based on no victimization. This was agreed. The union officials had previously stated that they would not meet the strikers if communists were present. The chairman of the strike committee put this to the meeting and it was unanimously agreed that they remain. The three full-time TGWU officials defended their position for abandoning the strike by repeating the stock phrases of 'unofficial action' and 'outside interference'. Nonetheless, the strikers gained some wage rates increases; trade union recognition; and the reinstatement of all dismissed strikers.

Elsewhere, 'in October 1936 the Scots herring women began a sudden and dramatic strike in East Anglia which in the end won them significant gains [...] the spectacle of several thousand non-unionized women bringing a complete industry to a halt was a sensation'.[84] The women were part of a large group of traditional itinerant gutters and packers and provided an unusual example of militant unofficial strikes in 1931, 1936, and again in 1938. Some of the women belonged to the TGWU and the union officials did negotiate on their behalf with the employers. The demand was for piece rate to be restored from 10d to 12d a barrel.

> So the girls struck [...]. [Y]ard after yard joined the strikers, and by seven o'clock practically the whole of the trade's intricate machinery was brought to a standstill. [...] Curers knew that even

81 TGWU 5/625 (BMW) Branch (2004), 'The 1934 Strike for Union Recognition at Pressed Steel: A Victory for the People of Oxford'.
82 Tim Claydon, 'Trade Unions, Employers and Industrial Relations in the British Motor Industry c. 1919–45', *Business History*, 1987, vol.29, no.3, pp.304–324.
83 R.C. Whiting, *Oxford: Studies in the History of a University Town Since 1800* (Manchester University Press, 1993), p.151.
84 Sam Davies, '"A Whirling Vortex of Women": The Strikes of Scots Herring Women in East Anglia in the 1930s and 1940s', 2010, *Labour History Review*, vol.75, no.2, pp.181–207, p.182.

if the strike lasted only until morning the position would be serious, for with the landings at their best for the season it was necessary to work into the night to catch up. [...] Forming themselves into long columns, ten deep, and linking arms, the strikers marched defiantly along the wharves and fish market, shouting a battle cry of 'We want a shilling a barrel'.[85]

The strike quickly spread from Yarmouth to Lowestoft with further demands for 17s 6d weekly rate and a limit of 12 hours on the working day. Local TGWU officials dealing with their male members in the curing trade were joined by more senior regional officers (*The Record*, November 1936). Later that day the strikers gathered outside the negotiations between the TGWU and the employers with some of the women's own representatives present. The TGWU officials asked the women to return to work as a precondition for any settlement. This was firmly rejected. The employers gave some ground and offered the 1s per barrel pay rise and the women's representatives accepted. Most of the strikers stayed out and hurled 'herrings and stones' at the police on guard in the pickling yards, and now demanded that the pay rise be both backdated and compensated for the days out on strike. These two points were quickly conceded, and again the TGWU urged the women back to work. This time they reluctantly agreed.

On the buses and trams forms of speed-up were also being imposed. In Glasgow all 31 branch secretaries of the TGWU were informed of changes to their duty sheets reducing meal times. The changes were notified to the men so late in the day by the union officials that there was no time to develop workplace resistance. On the London trams the employer wanted greater speeds on journey times. The TGWU members were worried by the excessive speeds, especially since many of vehicles were old and top heavy. The mood of the men was for strike action, but the TGWU officials dissuaded them.

Throughout the West Midlands there was organized opposition. The Birmingham trades council met to discuss Bedaux after the Hope strike, and Tom Roberts of the TGWU branch moved the resolution: 'That this conference uncompromisingly rejects the Bedaux system and as delegates pledge ourselves to return to the branches and factories in order to organise the greatest mass resistance to its introduction' (*Daily Worker*, 11 October 1933).

These disputes were the tip of an increasingly large iceberg of industrial militancy and class consciousness among younger workers, and in particular young women. This was part of an awakening among such groups, and the trade union leadership, despite its tendency to conservative inertia, was happy to recruit this growing band of labour into their

85   *Yarmouth Mercury*, 31 October 1936, cited in Davies pp.195–196.

ranks and accept their subs. Part of their opposition to management was low wages, but they also railed against greater exploitation through rationalization.[86]

A point emphasized by the unionization among women car workers was the relatively small numbers of women in factories run by Vauxhall, Ford, and Morris, were highly unionized with over 500 in the TGWU at Austin and over 200 at Standard Motors. The story unfolds of key women organizers, such as Freda and Gertie Nokes, at Longbridge.

> This surprising ease of recruitment is mirrored in the case of the Standard. In 1934 the women sewing machinists were laid off for a couple of weeks while new conveyors were put in the finishing shop and the shop reorganised. When they got back they were told that they would now have to do twice the amount of work for the same money. Kath Smith who had started working there a couple of years before, recalls: So there was a hue and cry over it, and one of the older girls said: '*Well why don't we join a union?*'.[87]

This chapter started with the economic slump, mass unemployment, and the election of a national government in 1931. It has described the huge impact of unemployment on the entire working-class movement, and the decision by the TGWU national leadership to follow a Mondist path industrially through collectively bargained arrangements with large employers and employers' federations, and politically by supporting a reformist approach to capitalism. It has ended with a series of accounts of worker resistance to imposed speed-up with the contradictory consequences that it served the purpose of the passive union leadership by recruiting members and winning bargaining rights.

---

86 Selina Todd, 'Boisterous Workers': Young Women, Industrial Rationalization and Workplace Militancy in Interwar England', 2003, *Labour History Review*, vol.68, no.3, pp.293–310.

87 Steve Tolliday, 'Militancy and Organisation: Women Workers and Trade Unions in the Motor Trades in the 1930s', *Oral History & Labour History*, 1983, vol.11, no.2, pp.42–55, p.43, emphasis added.

2

TGWU Policies and Sections in the 1930s

Introduction

This chapter looks at the TGWU in terms of its main sections – docks, road haulage, and passenger transport – and concludes with comments on Ireland and women members.

TGWU Sectional Development

The TGWU redoubled its efforts to recruit new members once the economy picked up. The union has been characterized as 'positive-expansionist' and 'one of the primary conditions for achieving relatively high union growth was thus a national leadership oriented and committed to growth as a priority'. In order to achieve this, the 'bifurcated' TGWU 'provided their general secretaries with a concentrated and centralized (in the non-bargaining channel) government eminently suitable for the purpose of influencing growth'.[1] While the points raised were for a later decade the argument remains true – that Bevin was able to force his policies through the layers of appointed officials and further into the lay ranks, hence the need to quell any rank-and-file opposition. This growth mantra hit many targets at once: financial security and organizational stability; influence over employers; influence within the TUC and Labour Party; and a power in the land.

In February 1937 Bevin gave his annual report on 'the work and structure of the union'. There were 13 geographical areas with 561,709 members as follows:

1 R. Undy, V. Ellis, W.E.J. McCarthy, and A.M. Halmos, 'The Development of UK Unions since 1960', in W.E.J. McCarthy (ed.), *Trade Unions* (Penguin, 1985), pp.281–282.

Area 1	London and the Home Counties	165,620
Area 2	South of England and Channel Islands	14,073
Area 3	West of England	38,004
Area 4	South Wales	32,646
Area 5	Midlands	50,203
Area 6	North West and North Wales	44,901
Area 7	Scotland	38,947
Area 8	North East	20,263
Area 9	Yorkshire and North Midlands	29,915
Area 10	East Coast	15,272
Area 11	Ireland	32,381
Area 12	Liverpool and Isle of Mann	35,095
Area 13	North Wales Quarrymen	18,958

plus 24,163 power workers, and 1,268 in central branches.

The membership was divided into eight national groups – docks, waterways, passenger road transport services, commercial road transport, power workers, metal engineering and chemical, clerical, and general. A ninth group representing the fishing industry was being established. The General group included food and drink, sugar beet, artificial silk, linen hosiery blankets, municipal non-trading, gas and electricity supply, civil engineering construction, cement clay chalk, and paint colour and varnish. There were two subdivisions – flour milling and agriculture, and building trade.

By 1938 the vast majority of the 122,000 employed workers in the docks, harbours, rivers and canals were in the TGWU. The great majority of the 198,000 tram and bus workers were in the union, as well as the bulk of the other 182,000 road transport workers. The tramway men and bus workers were well organized but the former were less militant. In contrast lorry drivers and carters tended to be weakly organized, although the TGWU was increasing its membership despite the difficulties of recruiting in large numbers of small firms. Dockworkers presented a problem which was a hard nut to crack organizationally on account of their casual employment. The union sought to secure the registration of port labour, in order to limit the number of irregular applicants for work, but the reduction in foreign trade prevented decasualization from being nearly as effective as was hoped. The union was better organized in larger ports with some gains in pay and conditions.

Each national group had a national committee and officers. The committee is elected every two years, meets quarterly, and is composed of members from each area trade group committee. They deal with pay and conditions, national organizing, benefits, and send a member to the EC.[2]

> The Transport and General Workers Union, with its very heterogeneous membership, has adopted a form of sectional organisation under which each important group possesses representative machinery of its own. Each section has, moreover, its own negotiating officers, and normally each section draws up its own programme and puts forward its own demands, subject to approval of the Executive Council representing the union as a whole. The sections have, however, no power to declare or conduct strikes, except where this is a specially delegated to them by the Executive Council which usually keeps the deciding authority in its own hands.[3]

Members were based in about 3,000 branches, roughly organized on trade and included branches in Malta and Gibraltar. The GEC serves for two years, meets quarterly, and appoints all officers except general and financial secretaries who are elected by ballot. Ultimate authority resides with the BDC. The union's success as an amalgamation is based on autonomy possessed by groups in trade matters; the pooling of resources with better research, legal, and political and friendly matters; all parts can help one another; larger organizations have greater influence in negotiations and with the public; and therefore there is powerful central direction and executive financial controls. A key factor is negotiated agreements through formal machinery giving rise to a strong centre rather than a loose federation. 'An outstanding feature of the Transport Union has been the opportunity afforded to the lay members for self-government. The Union is represented on 23 Joint Industrial Councils [...]. On 26 Trade Boards [...] on 14 Conciliation Boards [...] and on 2 Joint Councils'.[4]

The union finances were fully restored by 1936 – income was over £800,000 mainly from contributions (6d for men and 3d for women). Many of these benefits came from the amalgamation process, and this allowed it to sponsor eight MPs. It also had an information and research section, publicity department, monthly *Record*, education scheme, and owned Transport House.

Two groups stood out:

> One is formed by the dockers and waterside workers. They are pertinaciously group-conscious with a tradition of militancy and

---

2 Arthur Creech Jones, 'Transport and Trade Unionism', in Cole, *Trade Unionism*, pp.314–315.

3 Cole, *Trade Unionism*, pp.307–308.

4 Jones, *Transport*, p.318.

possessing, in many cases, special skills [...]. The other group consists of the London road passenger transport workers. This group is enigmatic [...]. London busmen together are excitable, volatile, and, like the dockers, group-conscious.[5]

The latter had their own constitutional role in the TGWU and a tradition of militancy. Organized around garages and depot canteens they were closely linked together. Other general workers inside the TGWU had distinctive characteristics such as agriculture, metal trades, building trades, and government workers, but they lacked militant traditions. Car and road haulage workers had a tendency to group cohesion and militancy but it remained under-developed. All these groups were difficult to integrate inside the TGWU and this made administration harder. Dockers and busmen needed constant reminders of the benefits of amalgamation, and 'Bevin found the problem troublesome, recurring, and incapable of complete solutions'.[6]

Bevin secured some improvements in these years for seafarers, provender millers, and 'C' licence holders in road haulage. Through the TGWU he negotiated a joint arrangement with the fish merchants and fish porters in Billingsgate. These efforts went alongside progress among dockers, bus and tramway men, Welsh tinplate workers, and millers. The TGWU grew in influence and reach as the recession ended and as the labour market tightened. Bevin's role was indeed central – his energy, grasp of detail, and reputation ('my word is my bond') stood directly and indirectly behind most deals with employers. Two caveats need to be made to this list of triumphs: first, the labour market upturn meant that the objective bargaining position of many workers had improved; and the setting up of joint negotiating committees at national and/or sector level did not always match the realities on the ground. Secondly, Bevin's energetic pursuance of such formal agreements was partly in response to the mounting pressure from rank-and-file militancy, which frightened employers into dealing with the TGWU leadership as a case of 'better the devil you know'.

TGWU growth came mainly from recruitment in previously weakly organized sectors, but there were a few mergers with small groups such as the Scottish Busmen's Union in 1934 and the National Winding and General Engineers' Society in 1933. By the 1935 BDC on the Isle of Man, the TGWU had nearly half a million members (about a tenth of all trade unionists). It was involved in hundreds of local disputes. In such cases skilled negotiators were as important as militant pressure.

5 Allen, *Trade Union Leadership*, p.57.
6 Allen, *Trade Union Leadership*, p.58.

Dockers

Dock work remained harsh and conditions were harsher still despite the piecemeal progress made by the union. Tough-minded employers backed by violent managers and some corrupt union men meant that 'the whole history of Dockland is one series of battles, because it was vile work [...] people were fighting for jobs – and I'm talking about dockers now – fighting for jobs, this is the proper history of Dockland'.[7]

Despite Bevin's personal involvement with dock work, the dockers from the start of the amalgamation in 1922 were famously troublesome. The complexities of industrial relations in the ports has been well documented, but the failure to resolve deep-seated and deeply resented working practices created a world within a world of political and industrial tensions. The previous volume has covered the 1923 strike by over 40,000 dockers against agreed wage cuts, and the 1926 trouble over the suspension of an official which led to expulsions and another attempt to launch a breakaway union. Both cases challenged the efficacy of the TGWU and illustrated the hard road to unity. The third secessionist movement came in Glasgow in 1931. It was Bevin's authoritarian methods that had angered many dockers over the years, and, '[i]n 1932, the TGWU suffered a final setback with the secession of Glasgow dockers to form the Scottish Transport and General Workers' Union (STGWU) [...]. [W]hat angered the Glasgow dockers was Bevin's obvious distrust of the ballot in union affairs'.[8]

There were other feeble attempts at breakaway unions which were dealt with by the TGWU. For example, Mr Welch – an official of the union in the North East – tried to set up a new union based on the 'Altogether Society'. He was seen as 'disloyal' and roundly condemned by Bevin.[9] It is one of the great fears of union leaders that some group will leave and form a separate and competitive union. Usually these are short-lived, but in a few cases they either thrive or cause great disruption. The TGWU was particularly prone to such schisms due to its varied membership and at times inappropriate representational structures.

In general, 'the shape of industrial relations in dockland has been determined by the haphazard growth of the ports and the correspondingly haphazard structure of employment and trade unionism'.[10] Most workers were either Irish navvies or men associated with river work in the days of sail – sailors, Polish refugees, and old soldiers. In London and Liverpool it was the Irish who formed the basis of the core workforce, and this created further divisions and dissent inside the local union. Typical disputes included one

7 John Bell, *Hello, Are You Working? Memories of the Thirties in the North East of England*, eds Keith Armstrong and Huw Beynon (Strong Words, 1977), pp.30–31.
8 David Wilson, *Dockers: The Impact of Industrial Change* (Fontana, 1972), p.81.
9 Building Trades Section minutes, 15 November 1934, Tyne and Wear.
10 Wilson, *Dockers*, p.29.

in Hull where hands wanted more money for loading the timber onto motor transport. The union officials were quick to intervene as the action spread, and, although the employers made some concessions, they and the TGWU officers were unhappy with the breach of the agreement by the hundreds of workers in the royal docks of Victoria, Alexandra, and King George.[11]

By 1931 31 major ports had registration schemes of which 25 were jointly controlled, but the fight against casualization was bitter and uneven. Who was included was sometimes vague and based on local custom and practice. Coal trimmers, for example, were excluded and in some areas cleaners and timber porters as well.

> This was the heart of the reformers problem. Casualism had to be defined and, between the wars, the area for definition was set out port by port by area and occupation. Of course, the process of definition took an unconscionably long time but the pace of national progress was governed by the most dilatory port. Ideally, Bevin could have used the authority of his union to get schemes accepted at progressive ports and force the recalcitrants into line. But the size of the TGWU belied its essential weakness in the docks.[12]

Although conditions on the docks had deteriorated during the slump, the union could point to degrees of resilience. There was a lightning strike in the summer of 1934 by 60 dockers at the Kirkcaldy docks. Rain had stopped work but instead of being allowed to finish the job, dockers were ordered to work on another boat. This was urgent as it had to be finished to catch the tide but pay would be at ordinary time when they had been working on piece rate. This work was now to be given to casual labour hired that day and these were not members of the union. The TGWU dockers refused to be transferred and immediately struck work, causing sympathy action and closure of the port. It was normal for men to continue to unload a boat before being finished, even in conditions of casual daily labour. Thus, as the port was anxious to allow the boat to depart, officials were 'kept running all over the docks in an effort to get the unemployed to scab on the dockers' (*Daily Worker* 23 August 1934). Trade union life was still fraught with hardship especially with the drop in trade, and places such as Teesside struggled to recruit. Sustained pressure did enable wages to increase by 1935 to their 1932 levels.

In 1934 trade remained variable with a falling off of the coal market reducing some forms of dock work. Failings in the export trade to Germany also meant a loss of work, especially in the gas coal trade. By early 1935 there was some pick up of work on River Wharves, and with strong demand

11 The *Hull Daily Mail*, 28 March 1935.
12 Wilson, *Dockers*, p.90.

for coke there was offsetting of lean days on dockside. As was usual when work was thin some employers would select 'preference men', thus driving others into taking industrial action. These specially selected gangs fared well while their fellow dockworkers stood idle. An upturn in steel manufacturing helped improve the level of work available on the docks, and this allowed for a small increase in piece rate in 1936. By the end of that year work was getting busier although with still a hit-and-miss element in some docks. This carried over into 1937 as the overall slump gave way to a rearmament led boom. Both dock and river wharf work improved with the summer being reported as 'an exceptionally good quarter'.[13]

As war approached, employment remained strong in 1938, with shipments of coal and coke increasing. In the summer things changed again, with exports slackening off with many collieries idle as coal production ground to a halt. This was aligned with the depression in the iron and steel trade which fed through to work on the docks and wharves. When war was declared, trade was totally disrupted and as government regulations came into force, so uncertainty and dislocation paralyzed much of the dockside work.

Strikes and various stoppages were commonplace as employers sought to cut back on gains made. There were wage cuts at Bowaters in Ellesmere Port late in 1934, typical underpayment of crane drivers at Clarence Wharf in Middlesbrough early in 1935, and later that year a dispute over the starting times of short sea traders in Cardiff. Two cases were reported as settled by the winter of 1936: 200 Ipswich dockers went on strike over the withdrawal by the employer of 3s 6d travelling allowance to go down river to unload grain boats. In Liverpool 200 strikers resumed work after an agreement on overtime pay to unload a boat at midnight that had been delayed by a gale.

The day-to-day working life of dockers and their associated trades meant a stream of variable demands according to the cargo, the weather, the effort and skill required, and the nature of the employer. These problems never diminished and, while providing the bread-and-butter of union negotiations, also created a haphazard pattern of collective bargaining. Troubles continued into the war years and beyond.

Road Haulage

It was in road haulage that the TGWU focused much of its attention. Bevin had started out as an organizer of carriers in Bristol, and the Road Traffic Acts of 1930 and 1933 established both licensing and hours

13 Docks and Waterways Trade Group Committee minutes, 1 July 1937, Middlesborough.

limitations. Enforcement remained a problem in such a highly fragmented and competitive sector. Many of the workers refused union membership through fear of bully bosses. The TGWU wanted a national wage rate and protected conditions, and set up a national council, with larger employers hoping to force the others into line. The employers, especially in the north, opposed but Bevin used his political influence to persuade the Ministry of Labour to set up a national conciliation board in March 1934. The formal machinery was in place but the reality on the roads did not match that aspiration.

It was a very tough industry to organize, but there were spectacular developments in the 1930s.[14] The industry had mushroomed after the war and there were very few controls. Wages, hours, and conditions of employment were in a chaotic state. This was a concern for both the workers and the travelling public as Britain's roads became busier and busier with the increasing mechanization of transport. Indeed, comparisons with the Wild West with cowboy employers were frequently made.[15]

This forced the government's hand, and the second report of the Royal Commission on Transport (Cmd 3416, 1929) was the basis for the 1930 Act with the start of vehicle licences, drivers' licences, maximum speeds for heavy-goods vehicles, limits on hours of work, and mechanical tests. The 1933 Act introduced a four-fold licensing classification with A and B being hire and reward. Smith suggests: 'TGWU policy had been to win the incorporation of a national wages board into the Act, but all the government conceded was that the Industrial Court [...] must take into account existing collective agreements in its assessment of fair wages'.[16] By 1933 the membership within the RTC group stagnated at about 40,000 members. TGWU officials fought to maintain the union despite employer attacks and workers' own fearfulness.

R.G. Witcher, TGWU Area 1 RTC secretary, complained that officers had to carry out bread-and-butter activities to keep the union going and therefore weakened their own efforts. In Liverpool, for example, by the winter of 1932 the union had to concede to employers' demands for pay cuts and the introduction of the 'accumulative' week hitherto opposed by the workforce. At least the Liverpool drivers fought against the cuts, but in London the employers' demands to end the 1924

14 These parallel developments in the USA with the teamsters under Daniel Tobin. Barry Eidlin, 'Upon This (Foundering) Rock': Minneapolis Teamsters and the Transformation of US Business Unionism, 1934–1941', *Labor History*, 2009, vol.50, no.3, pp.249–267.

15 Geoffrey Goodman, *The Awkward Warrior: Frank Cousins, His Life and Times* (Spokesman, 1984), p.32.

16 Paul Smith, 'The Road Haulage Industry 1918–1940: The Process of Unionization, Employers' Control, and Statutory Regulation', *Historical Studies in Industrial Relations*, 1997, vol.3, no.1, pp.49–80, p.65.

agreement and force a pay cut was met with little union resistance.[17] According to the Ministry of Labour's own reports, road haulage was characterized by weak unionization and absence of collective bargaining. The union was mainly absent in South Wales except Cardiff, and in the South West except for Bristol. Even in Birmingham the employers refused to enter into negotiations. In 1933 the dominant theme was wages decided between employers and individuals. This meant an anarchic market-based system in which pay rose from 1.6 per cent to 40.3 per cent within the ten companies running the heaviest vehicles. Most men worked between 48–62 hours per week. Overtime, holidays, holiday pay, casualization, and intimidation practices all varied from firm to firm, with no regulation.

Hard times for the union were noted in the North East region with a call to strengthen the union as the only way to prevent pay cuts, as the minutes of the RTP group read: 'we should extend our activities by endeavouring to enrol the employees of those operators, who up to the present, have been a menace to us because of low wages and shocking conditions they have been working under' (31 March 1932).

Pickford's Removals, based in Long Eaton, was one well-established local company organized by the TGWU. Trades unionism now began to re-establish a foothold, following the setting up of national controls over wages. Twenty-two drivers at Buoyant Upholstery works in Sandiacre were enrolled in mid-1933. 'Good results' on recruitment were seen in the Darley Dale area in 1934, and Brooks of the TGWU revealed that he knew of people 'in the industry who were contravening the law in every shape and form, but the (National Joint Conciliation) Board hoped in the course of a year or so to bring about such reforms as would make the industry one to be proud of'.[18]

The TGWU, from a position of weakness, demanded a national negotiating body. This was supported by the increasingly interventionist Ministry of Labour. The proposal was agreed although the government was lukewarm, but senior civil servants were more concerned with regulation and safety. A committee of four, including Bevin, was formed to 'advise' on pay and conditions. While the system was thoroughly voluntary it had been formed with some arm twisting by senior government officials. In March 1934, the National Joint Conciliation Board for the Road Transport Industry (Goods) for England and Wales was established and the same in Scotland. Bevin pushed hard for further developments now that the door was ajar. The TGWU launched a recruitment campaign with a *Lorry Driver's Special*. This resulted in growth of the RTC section to about 49,000, and later that year there

17 Smith, *Road Haulage*, p.67.
18 Taken from a case study by Graham Stevenson.

was an agreement on a three-grade wage classification with add-ons for London and long haul. While areas had some control over wages, other conditions remained national, such as 48-hour week, overtime, and holiday pay rates.

The TGWU's commitment was not matched by the divided employers, with non-compliance the norm. The RTC membership rose to 59,500 in 1935 due to both the employers' behaviour and a further membership drive. Union difficulties remained, with victimization of activists (at Maples for example), some business unions being set up as stooge organizations to keep out the TGWU (south east), and non-ratification (eastern). Bevin fought back, but according to Smith 'in effect, acceptance of the right to "sweat" labour was exchanged for a promise to regulate its price'.[19]

Bevin acknowledged the fundamental weakness of the RTC in terms of its bargaining position, and argued that he had at least established the principle of joint regulation even if the terms were currently inadequate. Out of this mess came the Bailie committee, set up by government after six out of ten area boards failed to reach any settlement.[20] This again showed the strengthening move towards state intervention in the name of both industrial peace and modernization of capital. While some gains had been made by the TGWU, Bevin and the section leadership realized that only a prolonged and bitter struggle could win more concessions. Statutory regulation seemed the better bet given the improvement in the economy and the European-wide trend to statism.

Frank Cousins (TGWU general secretary, 1956–1969) worked as a long-distance lorry driver in the 1930s, based in Doncaster. The industry was bedevilled by long hours, atrocious conditions, widespread pilfering, and rogue employers. His experiences on the road made him a union activist, and his first encounter with Bevin was at a meeting in Leeds where he shouted at the general secretary about the real difficulties of organizing. As a result – the story goes – he was appointed as a full-time official in 1938 by Bevin himself.[21] As Goodman says, his main tasks were recruitment and organizing: 'he still toured the lorry parks and transport cafes, which he knew well, keeping up the prescribed schedule of recruitment and indeed exceeding it. It was hard work, but he enjoyed it'.[22]

19 Smith, *Road Haulage*, p.71.
20 The Minister of Labour (Ernest Brown) said that this 'is a Bill to regulate the remuneration of workers employed by public, private and limited carriers who provide mechanical transport of goods by road. It directly affects 250,000 holders of licences and 500,000 vehicles, driven and attended by between 500,000 and 600,000 workers.' Hansard, HC Deb 11 May 1938 vol. 335 cc1611-571611.
21 Goodman, *Awkward Warrior*, p.41.
22 Goodman, *Awkward Warrior*, p.43.

Busmen in London and Elsewhere

Between 1932 and 1937, the busmen of London were indeed the major troublesome priests within the TGWU. They were well organized, had well-founded grievances, were well led mainly by communists, and would not allow the TGWU official machinery to bypass them in negotiations with the employer. As a result they were granted, from necessity rather than from principle, unusual rights to control their own destiny. This ended in 1937 with expulsions, bans, and the dismembering of their own organizations. Ken Fuller has provided an excellent account of these years as part of his wider examination of the bus workers' journey through struggle.[23]

> The London busmen have been for a long time the best organised and most militant section of the membership of the TGWU. The busmen are organised round their places of work – garages and depots. This type of shop organisation encourages militancy. It is the basis for shop stewards movement [...] its potentially explosive qualities, which were unlikely to commend it to right-wing Trade Union leaders in search of a quiet life.[24]

In contrast, busmen in the provinces were badly organized, and many companies refused to recognize the union or to bargain collectively with their employees. This improved by the late 1930s when the employers merged into larger groups.[25] The question remained:

> Why the London busmen should be one of the most militant industrial groups in the country is not, at first sight, easily explained. They suffered little from unemployment or the effect of the Depression; their average earnings were comparatively high; the London General Omnibus Company and its successor, the London Passenger Transport Board, were good employers and their conditions of work were better than in many industries.[26]

The 20,000 members exhibited a strong sense of solidarity based on tightly knit garage branches. They enjoyed a greater measure of self-determination (Anderton's Hotel Agreement[27]) through an elected Central London Area Bus Committee which had its own full-time secretary and a direct route to the union's GEC.

23 Fuller, *Radical Aristocrats*, pp.109–170.
24 Cole, *Trade Unionism*, pp.308–309.
25 Richard Temple, "'A Difficult and Peculiar Section": Provincial Bus Company Workers, 1934–47', *Labour History Review*, 2013, vol.78, no.2, pp.197–226, p.198.
26 Bullock, *Trade Union Leader*, p.519.
27 Hugh Clegg, *Labour Relations in London Transport* (Blackwell, 1950).

Figure 2: The Busman's Punch
Credit: TGWU archive at the Modern Records Centre
(MSS.126/TG/11/2/2)

The first skirmish was in 1932. The employer wanted to cut wages and jobs (about 800). Bevin tried to negotiate a better deal but one which still included job and wage cuts (*The Record*, August 1932). This seems odd for the 'good employer' described by Bullock. The men protested under the leadership of Bert Papworth (branch secretary at Chelverton Road). He helped to set up the Rank-and-File Committee, which in turn called a series of mass meetings with support from the *Daily Worker* and communist activists. In a ballot the vote against the employers' offer was won by 16,593 to 4,469 and the group asked the TGWU GEC to authorize strike action. 'Faced with this revolt, Bevin set to work to cut the ground from under the unofficial committee's feet by re-opening the negotiations'.[28] Under such pressure the employer made

28 Bullock, *Trade Union Leader*, p.520.

major concessions and this was signed off in late September. Bevin took the credit, claiming 'the success of the Union's negotiations on behalf of the London busmen' (*The Record*, October 1932), but Papworth and his supporters knew full well that it was their actions that had changed the decision. Despite attacking the strikers, Harold Clay could still argue that 'the employers have learnt the value of combination and national action on these matters which initially affect the industry. The workers must also see that it is in their interests to combine and take common action' (*The Record*, November 1932).

As a result the rank-and-file committees became permanent, with one in each affiliated garage. In January 1933 the Forest Gate garage went on strike against a negotiated schedule change. Within days the rank and file had organized solidarity action in over 20 other garages and with the tube workers at Morden. The men returned after an improved offer came from the employer, and as a result rank-and-file representatives won 10 of the 13 places available to the busmen for the Cambridge BDC in July.

At that conference the busmen were ready to take on Bevin, his supporters, and his overall world view. Frank Snelling spoke for them when he rejected Bevin's plans to end unemployment and pointed out that it was not the job of the TGWU to solve the problems of the bosses and of capitalism. Bevin was charged with 'Mondism', which was well founded. Papworth himself led accusations that the union was not standing up to fascism and argued in favour of the communist-inspired 'united front'. Bevin replied that he would not permit any undermining of official union structures and decision-making – a union within a union was unacceptable.

His anti-communism was more pragmatic than that of the TUC who wanted to stop communists from holding office. He did attack the unofficial strikers as 'union breakers' and believed this tactic to be part of the CP's activity to destroy the union itself (*The Record*, September 1933). He wished to squeeze out all contrary union initiatives partly to secure the integrity of the mergers and partly to reduce leftist opposition to his policies, both industrial and political. Eventually a breakaway union did emerge without communist support and was easily defeated.

'Busmen answer Mr Bevin', the *Daily Worker* (9 December 1933) reported after the election of five prominent activists to the TGWU's Central Bus Committee, the body that negotiated with London Passenger Transport Board for all uniformed staff. Militant activists were being widely elected at branch level to positions 'formerly filled by Mondist reactionaries'. With the aid of Emile Burns they established a news sheet, *The Busman's Punch*, around which the London busmen's rank-and-file movement was built. They always had difficulty in fitting in with the trade group system of the TGWU because of their own strong single union origins.[29]

29 Fuller, *Radical Aristocrats*, pp.19–35.

The employers were organized through garages, districts, divisions, and a central HQ. The union organization reflected this hierarchy, and made it easier for the CP to target this section.[30] Once the CP had gained a foothold it was obviously at odds with the TGWU GEC.[31] There was no compromise to be had, and therefore the only way for the union to restore control was through 'suspending the machinery, declaring the Movement subversive, and taking disciplinary action against its leading members'.[32]

Other busmen also took action in, for example, Glasgow in March 1937; in the Eastern Counties at Norwich, Cambridge, Cromer, and Newmarket in April and May; and in West Kent and East Sussex. The tale is told of strikes and solidarity action being repudiated by the TGWU officials among the London Green Line busmen who, along with colleagues in Slough, returned to work after being attacked by Bevin. His action backfired as other workers took strike action in protest including those in Luton, Leatherhead, Dorking, and Walton-on-Thames. In August 1935, 2,000 transport workers from West Wales took strike action over 'equal pay for equal work' in the 19 small bus companies. The local TGWU official, Andrew Murray, demanded on behalf of Bevin that the men give up their 'unofficial' strike. They unanimously refused.

In May 1937 the so-called 'Coronation' strike was played out on the streets of London, and resulted in suspensions and expulsions of the leaders of the rank-and-file movement (see Chapter 3).

The TGWU in Scotland, Wales, and the Island of Ireland

Most Scottish and Welsh unions were integrated with their English equivalents and largely shared their trials and tribulations. In Ireland things were somewhat different.

By 1937 there were an estimated 326,000 trade unionists affiliated to the Scottish Trade Union Congress (STUC). Most workers belonged to UK-wide unions with a very few Scottish only ones, mainly in textiles, building trades, printing, and baking. The Scottish Dockers' Union controlled Glasgow ports with about 1,000 members but remained outside the STUC. The TGWU had about 35,000 members in Scotland. Most workers remained on the poverty line, and 'without the Trade Unions and their activities Scotland might today be little better than a coolie plantation'.[33]

30 Allen, *Trade Union Leadership*, pp.63–73.
31 AJS (September 1935), 'The Strike Movement in Road Passenger Transport' (*Labour Monthly*).
32 Allen, *Trade Union Leadership*, p.65.
33 Thomas Johnston, 'Trade Unionism in Scotland', in Cole, *Trade Unionism*, p.231.

Scottish employers used the depression to cut wages. In the building trades, workers suffered long hours, low pay, and dangerous conditions. The TGWU tried to rally the members, and held the first Scottish delegate conference on 13–14 September 1932 in Glasgow. Scottish independence was part of the complication of securing backing for the TGWU's policy of establishing national agreements through centralized bargaining. Some of this was winning through, for example when the Scottish busmen joined the TGWU in 1934, and in late 1936 the Glasgow busmen were on strike over new duty sheets. By the time of the 1936 conference there were nearly 40,000 members of the TGWU in Scotland, and with the upturn in the economy this number rose by another 20,000 by the end of 1938. In early 1939 Bevin spoke at a meeting in Alloa where he called for public ownership of all transport, and made a plea for more women to join the union (*The Record*, February 1939). As trade developed by 1938, dockers were able to successfully negotiate extra payments for exceptional loads such as sugar at Greenock and cement at Ayr.

In North Wales trade unionism was weak among the tourist and agricultural sectors, and the TGWU region was combined with Cheshire. There was a concerted effort to recruit manual workers in local government with meetings and the setting up of numerous branches.[34] The 8,000 members of the North Wales Quarrymen's Union had recently merged with the TGWU bringing with them Welsh speaking officials and a strong commitment to union education.

In the cities of South Wales the TGWU had about 9,000 members in the dock and marine sections, was strong in passenger and commercial transport, and organized the lower skilled men in the shipyards. The TGWU was also the main union in the chemical and non-ferrous metals factories, and among flannel weavers, fishermen, trawler engineers, and flourmill workers. It was the second largest union in Wales after the MFGB, and under strong communist influence it worked with the Cardiff Trades Council and the South Wales Council of Action to back the unemployed marches and anti-fascist united front.

The TGWU was also the best organized and most representative union for women workers as with the rayon workers of Flint.[35] In 1933, with the slump hitting South Wales's working-class communities, the TGWU started a recruitment push in their main strongholds, and were able to win a rare pay rise for the spelter workers in Swansea Vale. In contrast the tinplate industry suffered badly from the downturn in world trade and by the summer of 1935 was in deep crisis. With the rise of Deakin, a proud adopted son of Wales, there was more urgency from the centre of the union towards the plight of the tinplate men (*The Record*, August 1938).

34 Huw Edwards, *It Was My Privilege* (Gee and Son, 1957).
35 H.A. Marquand, 'Trade Unionism in Wales', in Cole, *Trade Unionism*, p.240.

The TGWU organized throughout the island of Ireland in the 1930s, and remained strong in its traditional areas. The Amalgamated TGWU was so named to differentiate it from the Irish TGWU. At times its relationship with its parent union was stormy and litigious, although it remained firmly wedded to the link. Sectarian and nationalist divisions hampered all union activity and bedevilled working-class solidarity as well as union organization. The Amalgamated Transport and General Workers' Union (ATGWU) established important niches in employment both north and south of the border. Its core membership was in Derry among Catholic dockers and carters.

The ATGWU dominated Northern Ireland trade unionism, and had a higher dispute level than the south with, for example, the strike of 2,000 women in Ewart's Mill on the Crumlin Road. Their leader, Saidie Patterson became the first woman full-time officer in Ireland. She was

> a weaver at William Ewart's mill, took the opportunity afforded by the war conditions, and the consequent demand for linen, to lead a seven-week strike as part of a campaign by the Amalgamated Transport and General Workers' Union for a closed shop in the linen industry. In a speech she gave during the strike, Patterson explained that there were no trade boards or any other mechanism, to regulate wages in the industry, which is why they wanted 'a strong 100% trade union organisation, capable of demanding better conditions for the thousands of textile workers, instead of merely pleading for them'. The strike was unsuccessful, but Patterson believed that they had contributed to the battle for better conditions.[36]

Nonetheless,

> the most substantial strike in which the Union was involved in the 1930s was in Ireland where, surprisingly enough, the establishment of the Irish Free State had not driven the British unions out. This was a standing provocation to Irish nationalists, the more so as the stronghold of nationalism in the purely Irish trade unions was also a transport union which Jim Larkin had founded and led in the famous Dublin strike of 1913. Such union and national rivalries had as much to do with the twelve-week strike of the Dublin tramway men at the beginning of 1935 as any economic causes. The dispute cost the Union £24,000 in strike pay, but Bevin was determined to see it through if only to show that the ATGWU could be as militant as its Irish rival.[37]

36 www.acenturyofwomen.com
37 Bullock, *Trade Union Leader*, p.556.

In early 1935, the Dublin tramway men embarked on an expensive twelve-week strike. It started in early March in response to the sacking of a bus driver. It soon spread to include over 3,000 workers from both the ATGWU and the Irish Transport and General Workers' Union (ITGWU). Solidarity calls were made to the London-based TGWU rank-and-file bus committee to raise funds for their Dublin comrades. The Fianna Fáil government sent in the troops and the Irish Republican Army (IRA) pledged support to the strikers. The dispute heightened tensions within and between the unions, and became a battle ground for more than an industrial dispute over pay, conditions, and victimization. After eight weeks they voted to continue the strike despite efforts by the Anti-Communist League to weaken their resolve, and so the dispute entered Easter week fighting for the traditions of James Connolly.

The strike remained solid with both unions fighting together on the picket lines and in their determination to win. After 12 weeks, the longest transport strike in Irish history, the day was won.[38] Sam Kyle was the union's man on the spot, and he was pulled and pushed by the strikers, the employers, and the Irish government. He followed Bevin's privately conveyed advice that the strikers 'sit tight' in which case the company and the government would begin to wonder what was happening and about to happen. He warned against 'chasing' the dispute and also that the 'men' should hold their nerve and accept whatever deal the union negotiates. And so it was.

In early 1932 there was a dispute at the Sirocco works in Belfast, and this was part of a wider picture of fights against pay cuts which persuaded Bevin to visit the textile industry members amid calls for unity. In June 1932 there was an all-Ireland ATGWU conference in Cork. The union president (Herbert Kershaw) made a plea for unity: 'whatever our race, colour or religion, there is one economic problem which has to be faced and which calls for the absolute unity of the working class', namely the failure of capitalism (*The Record*, July 1932). In October 1934 the conference was held in Belfast and Bevin used it to attack both enemies outside the movement in the form of fascists, and those inside the movement, such as the ITGWU, whom he accused of splitting the fight back.

In the summer of 1935 there was a more disturbing dispute sparked by attacks on Catholic workers in Belfast. Although the official trade union line was to condemn all such attacks, there were reactive strikes and riots in Limerick, Galway, Sligo, and Waterford.[39] Galway had been a backwater of industrialization and as such, trade unionism was thin on the ground until the 1920s. It was the ITGWU that started the ball rolling after the Great

---

38 Bill McCamley, *The Role of the Rank and File in the 1935 Dublin Tram and Bus Strike* (Labour History Workshop, 1981).
39 Brian Hanley, 'Galway's Wildcat Strike', *The Irish Story*, 14 January 2013.

War, based substantially on an anti-English ticket. In June 1933, with a building boom in progress, the ATGWU sought to develop its strength locally and called a strike of its 700 members to force employers to use union-only labour.[40]

Hanley notes: 'late July 1935 saw an unprecedented wave of anti-Protestant activity in the Irish Free State. Emotions ran high after a week of violence in Belfast where several people were killed and dozens injured in rioting after Orange parades. Catholics were forced from their homes and workplaces and several were killed'.[41] In response there were violent anti-Protestant attacks in Limerick on 20 July, and a few days later there were unofficial strikes in Galway demanding the dismissal of all Protestant workers. Over the next few days there were arson and gun attacks on the homes, businesses, and places of worship of Protestants. The Garda reluctantly provided some protection, but the official line was that the attacks were carried out by local drunks. The Irish fascists, the 'Blueshirts', were blamed for the more violent incidents.

ATGWU union members in Galway went on unofficial strike 'until every Orange workman no matter who he is, [was] cleared out'.

On Monday July 22nd dock workers in Galway refused to unload a cargo of grain from the S.S. Comber, a ship owned by Sir William Kelly of Belfast. The vessel was boarded and its ensign taken down and burnt, while the crew were informed that it would be safer for them not to leave the ship. The leaders of the action, William Carrick and John Healy, were both officials of the Amalgamated Transport and General Workers Union and Labour Party members of Galway Urban Council.[42]

The strike leaders held a rally where they called for a general strike to drive all Orangemen out of town. They demanded that all Catholic workers strike until this was achieved. The dockers and others marched through the town, and again on 23 July the dockers stopped work until a Protestant chief engineer disembarked. The dockers then called upon local engineering workers to join them as did over 50 women from the local laundry. The strikers marched around the town calling for support and this led to several confrontations with other workers and the police. The Republican Congress lamented how 'two councillors-members of the ATGWU, are inciting against Protestants, attempting to secure their

40 John Cunningham, 'A Great Believer in the "Internationale": A British Trade Union in Galway 1911–1936', 2015, *Academia.edu*, online article, p.13.
41 Hanley, 'Galway's Wildcat Strike'.
42 Hanley's article is based on reports from the *Connacht Tribune, Connacht Sentinel, Irish Times,* and Garda.

dismissal'.[43] The CP accused the strike leaders of 'imitating' the Ulster Unionists and called on workers to resist efforts to 'foment a counter-pogrom' against Protestants. When approached by the Republican Congress, ATGWU officers in Dublin pleaded ignorance of the dispute.

Such fraught episodes, while rare, showed the additional tensions inside the British-based unions when confronted with a mixture of sectarian and industrial issues with a backdrop of recession. Nonetheless, the union was hard pressed to control its Irish cohorts, and when push came to violent shove, Bevin and the national leadership backed its Irish officials and members in order to keep some credibility in the face of stern competition from its rival transport union. Elsewhere in Ireland the ATGWU continued to make progress with the recruitment into its ranks of Ulster linen workers in late 1936, and with support for the Cork building workers' wage dispute in the autumn of 1937. By the time of the June 1938 conference at Portrush membership had again risen in line with the economic recovery.

Women Workers in the TGWU

In 1938 there were 802,000 women in unions of whom 451,000 were affiliated to the TUC. The largest groups were in professional and public services – teachers, civil servants, and municipal clerks. The largest industrial group was in textiles (230,000) of whom 162,000 were cotton operatives. There were only three small all-women unions affiliated to the TUC. Generally they paid lower subs but were eligible for the same services as men. Nonetheless, 'women have proved beyond question their capacity to organise, and individuals have shown conspicuous qualities of leadership, but women are nevertheless relatively weak in trade union organisation and play a minor part in trade union councils'.[44]

A major reason was that most women workers were under 25 since the marriage bar was maintained in many sectors. This problem was raised as a major issue at women's group meetings as it resulted in lower wages due to shorter hours, being younger, and lower piece rate. In the early 1930s more women went to work, especially in the new industries such as engineering.

Throughout the 1930s the TGWU position on its women members changed dramatically. It went from little interest and a rather patronizing tone to a full-on appreciation of their rights and the contribution they were making to the labour movement. This shift was mainly

---

43 Republican Congress minutes, 27 July 1935, cited in Hanley, 'Galway's Wildcat Strike'.
44 Barbara Drake, 'Women in Trade Unions', in Cole, *Trade Unionism*, pp.249–261, p.253.

accomplished through the efforts of women members and activists themselves. The TGWU officially opposed the marriage bar (*The Record*, February 1932), and as we have seen, many women strikers were in the TGWU. By 1934 the 'women's' section of *The Record* took on a more serious note with attacks on fascism and with deep concerns about deaths in childbirth. Under communist influence, key figures in the TGWU took a strong line against Franco's putsch in Spain, and women members played vital roles in raising support and aid for the Republic (*The Record*, November 1936).

In the March 1937 edition of *The Record*, Bevin made a special plea to women to join the union, especially in the growth of industries of the Midlands. He stressed the benefits of being unionized, and added the extra features of union services available to women members. Indeed, the union went about recruiting women as trade unionists and not, as previously, as helpers.

The shift from home working to the factories meant that 'the real conflict of the time is the struggle of these various classes, some working in factories, some working in their homes, to maintain a standard of life'.[45] The role of women in both the transition to factory work and in forming worker combinations was stark and clear. This tradition was handed down to those fighting in the 1930s, and, as we have seen, women, especially young women, played a major part in a variety of strikes and used these actions to recruit union members. Without them the TGWU leadership would have remained indifferent to the lot of women workers. A piece for *The Record* (February 1938) recognized the role of 'women workers and trade unionism' urging a membership push as well as emphasizing the benefits in terms of wages, conditions, and a range of health and safety issues.

Most women, married and unmarried, have always worked both in cluster occupations around textiles and in the home with housekeeping and child rearing.[46] It was with industrialization, when women entered factory life as wage earners that a wider, usually hostile, commentary arose about such work being 'unnatural' and 'immoral'.[47] It was war, however, rather than factories that changed women's role as wage earners. The impact of industrialization meant more paid work for women, but 'prelapsarians' saw the factories as killing a more 'wholesome' way of life. More fundamental was the view that poverty drove women into all and any form

45 J.L. and Barbara Hammond, *The Town Labourer 1760–1832* (Longmans, 1917), p.18.

46 Elizabeth Roberts, 'Women's Work 1840–1940', in Leslie Clarkson (ed.), *British Trade Union and Labour History: A Compendium* (Macmillan, 1990), pp.209–280.

47 Janet Greenless, 'Women and Work in Inter-war Lancashire', *Historical Studies in Industrial Relations*, 2002, vol.13, no.1, pp.119–136; a review of Miriam Glucksmann, *Cottons and Casuals: The Gendered Organisation of Labour in Time and Space* (Sociology Press, 2000).

of employment, and as such created a unitary working-class approach to survival and the making of the working class as a class in and of itself.

There have been a range of important, but usually inconclusive, studies on the exact numbers of women involved in waged work by age, sector, region, and wage levels. In 1935, for example, female earnings as a percentage of male co-workers ranged from 55 per cent in textiles to 37 per cent in paper and printing.[48] It was still the case that 'married women who worked full-time incurred a great deal of criticism throughout the period'.[49] The only way to resolve the conundrum of the link between lower pay and critical commentaries, was, of course, to fight for higher wages, equal wages, and to do so through a strategic approach based on trade union principles. Views were contradictory – some men supported women at work to help family finances and as a right, but others saw them as a threat to wage levels. This was partly an acceptance of the widely held, but wrong, wage fund thesis that the total amount of money available for wages was static and therefore that the more people sharing it, the thinner each slice.

Many women themselves had ambiguous attitudes to work and working. Historians are divided as between those decrying the lack of women active in trade unions,[50] while others applauded those that did join unions and took up the fight.[51] All agree that women fought shoulder to shoulder with each other and men in union organization and disputes, and that once most unions were open to women members then the main problem was not union membership but continuity of employment itself. Most oral history records women more than willing to take on their employers, especially when confronted with bullying from supervisors and overseers.

Despite grudging support from TGWU leaders, women joined up and joined in, especially in the Midland-based factories such as Lucas, Cadbury, GEC, and Courtaulds. Women took leading roles in strikes against speed-up as noted, but they were also key figures in the strike at Burndept Wireless in Kent. This was a wages struggle, but crucially linked to facilities associated with the dirty job of making batteries. This combination of winning issues ignored by male managers and union officials allowed for the mass recruitment of women into the TGWU.[52]

48 Jane Lewis, *Women in England 1870–1950: Sexual Divisions and Social Change* (Indiana University Press, 1984).
49 Roberts, *Women's Work*, p.244.
50 Sheila Lewenhak, *Women and Trade Unions* (E. Benn, 1977).
51 Deborah Thom, 'The Bundle of Sticks: Women Trade Unionists and Collective Organisation Before 1918', in Angela John (ed.), *Unequal Opportunities: Women's Employment in England 1800–1918* (Blackwell, 1986), pp.261–285.
52 Dorothy Jacques (December 1937), 'Women Workers in a Wireless Factory' (*Labour Monthly*).

Women did join unions in the car industry and their embracing of strike action, and their militancy per head was more than that of men.[53] Faced with employers handing large numbers of women on a metaphorical plate to the TGWU, Florence Hancock was brought in as a women's organizer. In 1935, she joined the GEC, and served as the chief women's officer from 1942. Central was the campaign for equal pay, and the TGWU took to the radio in the form of Harold Clay to argue the case before a national audience (*The Record*, January 1938). By the 1939 BDC at Bridlington, the TGWU leadership was issuing a special call for women to join up.

This chapter has described the TGWU's approach to collective bargaining in terms of accommodation with the growing concentration of capital and with the greater intervention of the state. At times its leaders seemed more interested in quelling its own dissidents than in fighting the employers, and this theme carried it through the early 1930s as a union of passive resistance and beset with anti-communist dogma. There were varied outcomes in terms of union influence and improvements for members. The main focus has been on those groups associated with the mainstream of the union's struggles – the dockers, road haulage, and the London busmen. In all cases progress was hard, and internecine warfare weakened the union and distracted it from core issues. While there were special issues throughout Ireland, the same analysis held. Women were an increasingly important part of such developments, but were met with indifference and hostility despite some official support.

It is fitting that this chapter ends with the 1935 general election victory of the Conservatives, and the revival of the Labour Party.[54] In October the labour movement had no real choices left. It endorsed both rearmament and the use of might to enforce League of Nation's sanctions, paving the way for war. It was the newly elected communist MP, William Gallacher, who emphasized 'working-class struggle'.[55] His maiden speech in the House of Commons on 4 December 1935 focused on the evils of imperialism and those that supported it, and he called for a 'Government that follows the road of peace and progress' and warned those who would block its path 'will have to pay a price far beyond any present reckoning'.[56] Tragically that was not the government in Westminster during the run up to war.

53   Knowles, *Strikes*, pp.182–184.
54   John Saville, *The Labour Movement in Britain* (Faber and Faber, 1988).
55   William Gallacher, *Revolt on the Clyde* (Lawrence & Wishart, 1936), p.1.
56   Gallacher, *Revolt*, p.296.

3

1936–1939:
Rearmament, Recovery, and the Fight Against Fascism

Introduction

This chapter examines the TGWU's collective bargaining strategy; its fight against fascism at home and abroad; its educational provision; and its involvement in the rearmament debate.

In October 1936 Harry Pollitt, general secretary of the Communist Party of Great Britain (CPGB), attacked the position of the Labour Party and the TUC:

> At a moment of most serious crisis, when workers expected a clear, straightforward lead, the Labour Party Conference at Edinburgh adopted [...]a policy on every urgent issue that is not simply ambiguous and confusing but reactionary and dangerous to the whole future of the working-class movement.[1]

He meant the failure to form a United Front against fascism at home and abroad, the failure to support the NUWM, the continuing support for British colonialism, the absence of equality measures for women, and the dire acceptance of 'rationalization' of work. In this regard popular opinion was increasingly aired in the national media, with the *Daily Herald* and the *Daily Worker* of major importance in disseminating left arguments. The former had nearly two million readers at its height and was a useful vehicle through which labour leaders could fight off the worst attacks from the resurgent right of British politics. The battle for ideas among left-wing rivals intensified, and found more outlets for their ideas and programmes through the founding of the Left Book Club and Penguin Books. Both reached large markets among working-class activists thirsting for readable debates.

---

1 Harry Pollitt, *Articles and Speeches 1936–1939* (Lawrence & Wishart, 1954), p.19.

Several socialists poured scorn on the idea, endorsed by the TGWU leadership that the main purpose of the trade union movement was to help capitalists make a bigger cake:

> According to this theory, the workers and the capitalists both make a 'national cake' and both are therefore entitled to receive a 'slice' of it. The only way we can get a thicker slice is to make a bigger cake. Otherwise, if some get a thicker slice, it can only be at the expense of others.[2]

This imagery was used by Labour chancellor Stafford Cripps in the 1940s and by Conservative prime minister Margaret Thatcher in the 1980s. It is also the main argument that Bevin fought for inside the TGWU, namely that the job of the unions was to negotiate 'a fair day's pay for a fair day's work'.

Big, Bigger, and Biggest

The hallmark of Bevin's strategy was to build a big union to match bigger corporations and growing state intervention. In other words the growth of large-scale capitalist enterprises brought forth large unions, and as these faced off so the state played its hand in helping capitalist production by controlling strong unions. Once the efficacy of large unionism became apparent in terms of dealings with both senior managers in corporations and senior mandarins in Whitehall, then the TGWU was to become the leading example of size matters. Just as the war was starting Deakin was calling for more efforts to build the union, and asked 'why not a million members?' (*The Record*, September 1939).

This was not always a straightforward proposition since in many sectors of the TGWU, such as in the building trades, there was already a three-way split in terms of active unions. With nearly 40 per cent of the workforce in no union at all the destructive inter-union rivalry was seen as a tragic weakness. Bevin's drive to dominate the sector and other industries led to the rise of inter-union agreements helpful to the TGWU. Eventually, such tactics led to the TUC developing the rules (Bridlington) to police such antics.[3]

In order to keep growing there had to be a hard central core of leaders broking no dissent as well as membership development and total opposition to any breakaways as with the Glasgow dockers and London busmen. This required support from the political wing of the movement, and Bevin's

---

2 William Gallacher, *The Case for Communism* (Penguin, 1949), p.170.
3 Lovell and Roberts, *TUC*, pp.142–143.

links with Citrine and the PLP meant the capture of such institutional vehicles to promote their brand of union building.

The Slide to War

The general election on 14 November 1935 had returned the national government under Baldwin. With some economic winds in their sails, a shifting national mood towards rearmament, and an ever fractious working-class revolt, the government lurched from constitutional debacles over the monarchy to foreign policy crisis over the Spanish civil war. By 1936 there was no doubt as to the nature and intentions of the fascistic regimes in Germany and Italy, alongside right-wing nationalists in Japan, Hungary, Rumania, and the insurgent Franco in Spain. Their growing aggression created a political crisis of appeasement among British Conservatives and splits in the labour movement of how best to treat such a monstrous ideology.

The TGWU leaders and activists were totally opposed to fascism in all its forms. Much of their rhetoric was aimed at all dictatorships and counterposed to the democratic traditions in Britain and among the labour movement. Once Hitler was in power there was 'no turning back' as the Nazis murdered socialists and trade unionists indiscriminately. The TGWU official line was also strongly anti-racist, and deplored outbreaks of anti-Semitism among its London taxicab members (*The Record*, May 1933).

Delegates at the BDC in 1935 launched a fierce attack on the fascists and warned of war to come. They also had no doubts about the nature of the British Union of Fascists (BUF) as they reported 'blackshirt brutality in West Ham' that autumn. In February 1936 the viewpoint from *The Record* was that German workers were now 'the serfs of the Junkers'. As the union celebrated Bevin's 25 years as a union officer, so the calls for a war economy grew. They knew that Hitler was a warmonger and were dismayed by cold feet and faint hearts among some Labour Party grandees.

The reaction of the TGWU to the Spanish civil war was generally to back the Republic, although in a somewhat tardy and hesitant manner. This was not the case when dealing with home-grown fascists, and the union constantly urged the government to stamp out the BUF. The union was furious with Chamberlain's open support for Mussolini and repudiated the Munich deals with Hitler in 1938. By now the full horrors of living under Nazi rule were apparent from the early use of concentration camps to torture and murder trade unionists, communists, Jews, all non-whites, the disabled, pacifists, and anyone else on the wrong side of their political and racial hatreds.

The problem remained, however, that the TGWU leaders still wished to plough a lonely furrow with refusal to join in the United and Popular Front anti-fascist coalitions. Its strong anti-fascist language was not matched by deeds. This mattered and further divided the TGWU membership with regard to fighting the fascists in the streets and on the battlefields of Spain.

In 1936 Britain was inching towards a new war economy. The first moves to budget for rearmament came with bomber command and the Royal Air Force. Metal replaced wood as the main material in the aircraft industry, and as a result 'this brought both problems and opportunities for the workers'.[4]

When George V died on 20 January 1936 he was briefly succeeded by Edward VIII. He had abdicated by December that year after various marital and political scandals, and was followed by George VI on 12 May 1937. A few weeks later Baldwin gave way to Neville Chamberlain. He in turn was handed a fistful of troubles from the new Irish constitution to Palestine, and from the Spanish civil war to appeasement his foreign affairs in-tray was full, and his domestic agenda in tatters.

In the summer of 1936 the TUC shifted to a more pro-war and rearmament position prompted by Hitler's move into the Rhineland, and growing doubts as to the effectiveness of the League of Nations. At the 1936 TUC congress in Plymouth the GC favoured non-intervention in the Spanish civil war, and opposed support for the Popular Front at home. Bevin was a major figure in this, and by the time of the 1937 TUC congress in Norwich Bevin was TUC president. His alliance with Citrine, and Dalton from Labour, made up a formidable front on foreign policy with backing for full rearmament alongside stronger resistance to fascism. The 1938 Blackpool congress recalled a lack of progress in terms of collective bargaining reach, and the movement was stuck with a government as insincere in terms of reform as it was craven in the face of Nazism.

The damaging ambiguity of the British ruling class towards fascism was showcased in the diaries of Chips Channon on pro-Nazi upper classes.[5] This 'collective scoundrelism' pervaded the deeply corrupt upper echelons of British political and social life.[6] They also supported the 1936 Berlin Olympics. The American Federation of Labor, in contrast, wanted a boycott of the games, but no such movement was apparent among British trade unions and the TGWU leadership were silent on this matter.[7] In 1938 the English football team playing Germany in Berlin, under orders from the government, took the Nazi salute.

4 Edmund and Ruth Frow, *Shop Stewards and Workshop Struggles* (Working Class Movement Library, 1980), p.10.

5 Henry Chips Channon, *The Diaries 1918–1938*, Simon Heffer (ed.) (Hutchinson, 2021).

6 G.B. Shaw, *Everybody's Political What's What* (Constable, 1944), pp.332–336.

7 Allen Guttmann, 'The "Nazi Olympics" and the American Boycott Controversy', in Pierre Arnaud and James Riordan (eds), *Sport and International Politics: The Impact of Fascism and Communism on Sport* (Taylor and Francis, 2002), pp.31–50.

'Tear the Fascists Down'[8]: United and Popular Fronts, and the Spanish Civil War

It was the Spanish civil war that defined a generation of socialists. Under pressure from pro-Franco Catholics the labour movement did not swing fully behind the defenders of another faith – those who believed in humanity and democracy.

> These years included the struggle against Mosley fascism at home and Franquist fascism abroad – the T&G was prominent. Thousands of British workers went to fight for the Spanish republic as part of the International Brigades, convinced that unless fascism was stopped in Spain, it would advance elsewhere. Although the Spanish republic was defeated and it took a world war to stop fascism in the end, the heroism of the International Brigades, which included in their number subsequent T&G general secretary Jack Jones, remains celebrated. A memorial to their bravery is on display in Transport House. (UNITE website)

United front politics, the call for anti-fascist unity, was an obvious response as fascism treated all its enemies the same (communists, socialists, liberals, democrats). It was 'the communists [...] who turned themselves into the most systematic and, as usual, the most efficient, champions of anti-fascist unity'. The United Front was labour-movement based and would become the Popular Front with allies from democrats and liberals. 'Anti-fascism, therefore, organized the traditional adversaries of the Right, but did not swell their numbers, it mobilized minorities more easily than majorities'.[9] The newly elected socialist government had won on promises to reform land use, enact greater social justice, and restrain the power of the Church, all of which was anathema to the reactionary powers behind the military. This is the heart of the matter that the Spanish CP perfectly understood, and that is why it is important to refute revisionist efforts to reinstate Orwell's misleading accounts of the civil war and the role of the communists.[10] In March 1936 transport workers in London showed how to fight fascists with details of a counter demonstration against the Blackshirts printed in the *Busman's Punch*, and with calls to all rank-and-file affiliated branches to join in backed by the rank-and-file leaders, Papworth, Sheehan, and Bailey.

---

8 Woody Guthrie song. He inscribed his guitar with 'this machine kills fascists'.

9 Hobsbawm, *Age of Extremes*, pp.147–149.

10 Tom Sibley, Introduction to *Two Pamphlets from the Spanish Civil War* (Manifesto Press, 2019).

The attitudes of the TGWU leadership towards Jews in general and Zionism in particular were mixed. The TGWU official policy condemned the overt anti-Semitism of the Blackshirts and at the 1933 BDC denounced Hitler and all his works. After the 1935 general election, the right-wing of the Conservative Party became bolder in its support for the fascists. The *Daily Express* spoke highly of Mussolini, and the *Daily Mail* cried 'hurrah for the blackshirts'. Bevin attacked the government's failings in their dealings with the fascists and even criticized the Labour Party leadership for not being more anti-fascist (*The Record*, October 1936). The TGWU understood that 'fascists destroy trade unions everywhere and will do so here' (*The Record*, March 1937).

While the TGWU leaders denounced the increasingly vile attacks on the Jews from the BUF and sections of the press, yet there remained a deep ambiguity in their general approach. Bevin in a series of speeches and articles showed sympathy for the Jews but became rambling and muddled when he spoke of their homeland in Palestine, and of how maybe they would all be better off in the land of their ancestors. This deep ignorance of such matters created a policy mess within the labour movement, and proved historically damaging when Bevin became foreign secretary in charge of the creation of the state of Israel.

The strong Catholic representation among many of the TGWU groups and regions meant a tendency to support Franco when civil war broke out in Spain. The Spanish civil war 'raised the fundamental political issues of the time: on the one side, democracy and social revolution, [...] on the other, a uniquely uncompromising camp of counter-revolution or reaction, inspired by the Catholic Church which rejected everything that had happened in the world since Martin Luther'.[11] The election victory in 1936 of the left alliance in Spain brought forth a military coup on 17 July. While Mussolini helped Franco, the British and others did not help the Republic.

Large numbers of foreign supporters formed the International Brigade (IB) which represented the historic moment of truth: 'Eventually over forty thousand young foreigners from over fifty nations (10,000 French; 7000 Jews; and 2000 British plus Americans, Germans, Austrian) went to fight and many to die'.[12] A pure and compelling cause, but the Republic was politically divided and without a single strategic military command. Franco had both unity and control. The history of the war and the story of the International Brigade have been told elsewhere,[13] but the TGWU leadership dithered and doubted when it mattered most.

11 Hobsbawm, *Age of Extremes*, pp.156–157.
12 Hobsbawm, *Age of Extremes*, p.160.
13 Tom Buchanan, *The Spanish Civil War and the British Labour Movement* (Cambridge University Press, 1991).

Many score of TGWU members joined up. Jimmy Moore was one example of a TGWU activist who died aged 21 in the conflict. He was a delegate to Portsmouth Trades Council. He wrote from his hospital bed having been mortally wounded at the battle of Ebro, 'I believe if the people of Portsmouth only knew the true conditions in Spain, they would rally together with the other people of England to see that the embargo was lifted from Republican Spain, and allow then to exterminate these Fascists invaders'.[14]

Meanwhile, in Ireland, despite official backing for donations for medical relief for Spain, increasing numbers of ATGWU members were against supporting the Republic: citing them as 'church burners and convent raiders'.[15] In contrast men like Bob Doyle, a Dubliner, fought in Spain aged 21 and was taken prisoner; and William Tumilson, a Belfast man, died at Jarma in March 1937 aged 33. This divide between the anti-fascists in Ireland and their nationalist enemies ran deep and hindered a united trade union response to the dangers ahead.[16]

Bevin and Citrine carry a heavy responsibility for their failings even as the Plymouth TUC endorsed this line. The Association of Catholic Trade Unionists, including inside the TGWU, was a powerful pressure group organized along the same lines as the Catholic Church and vehemently anti-communist.[17] Britain and France maintained their non-interventionist stance. It was the Communist International that mobilized as best it could with Tito as the recruiter-in-chief based in Paris and Togliatti aiding the Spanish CP, while Soviet military leaders did help with fighting in the theatre of war.

Bevin supported the Republic against the fascist Franco, but he followed Blum's lead from France and sucked up non-intervention. On 11 September 1936 the TUC debate saw both Bevin and Citrine denouncing the fascists, lamenting the fate of fellow workers, but remaining steadfastly committed to neutrality and non-intervention. It was Bevin who formally requested the TUC support for the National Council of Labour's policy.[18] As the farce of non-intervention was exposed, and after the Spanish delegates had made a passionate plea for support at the LP conference, Bevin began to reassess the TGWU's untenable position. In December he told the TGWU EC that we needed to rearm to fight

14 Alan Lloyd's eulogy at his memorial.
15 *Irish Independent*, 16 September 1936, quoted in Cunningham, 'A Great Believer', p.15.
16 'No Pasaran': Unite's Legacy Unions in Ireland and the Spanish Civil War (Unite History Project, 2016). Thanks to Alex Klemm for providing copy.
17 Knowles, *Strikes*, p.57.
18 General Secretary quarterly report, December 1936, cited in Bullock, *Trade Union Leader*, p.588.

fascism.[19] In March 1937 he reported to the TGWU EC that '[f]rom the day Hitler came to power, I have felt that the democratic countries would have to face war'.[20] The *Daily Worker* reported on 18 March 1937:

> ERNEST BEVIN has definitely disgraced the whole British trade union movement by sending away the Spanish delegates empty handed [...]. We declare that democracy is being sabotaged not only by Fascism, but also by our own trade union leaders.

In 1937 the labour movement inched towards the possibility of war and the need to rearm. In this the Spanish war had been the central catalyst. This corresponded with the call for a Popular Front which the TGWU leaders opposed. Bevin in an exchange of letters with G.D.H. Cole (January 1937) said 'joining up with the Communists who are out to destroy the trade unions [...] [is] asking too much'.[21] No ambiguity there.

Jack Jones (TGWU general secretary 1968–1977) was a young TGWU activist in Liverpool at the time. He was desperate to join the fight in Spain but was told he was needed as a TGWU organizer among dockers and seamen.[22] He was active in support of the Republic but 'was disappointed by the efforts of my own union and the TUC. Financial support from that quarter was negligible. I had the feeling that people in high places were washing their hands of the whole business'.[23] Jones recounts his meeting with Bevin once he had decided to join the IB in Spain. Bevin was supportive of his decision but remained pessimistic and limited in his view of the struggles to come. Jones's own account of his time with the IB, being wounded, and returning home show the lasting impact of the struggle as he recalled:

> with the end of the campaign, my wounds having healed, I returned to the docks and my own community. I was quickly back in the world of ships and cargoes and the human problems of the waterfront. Piece-work issues meant that there was no lack of involvement in union affairs and members welcomed me back as a mate and, for many, as a spokesman in adversity.[24]

The TGWU was not short on words of condemnation of the Spanish fascists and support for the Republican cause. As they said, 'their fight

19 General Secretary quarterly report, December 1936, cited in Bullock, *Trade Union Leader*, p.588.
20 General Secretary quarterly report, March 1937, cited in Bullock, *Trade Union Leader*, p.592.
21 Cited in Bullock, *Trade Union Leader*, p.596.
22 Jack Jones, *Jack Jones: Union Man, An Autobiography* (Collins, 1986), p.56.
23 Jones, *Jack Jones*, p.59.
24 Jones, *Jack Jones*, p.81.

is our fight' (*The Record*, September 1936), but they did not fight. On 26 April 1937 Franco ordered the bombing of Guernica by the Nazi Luftwaffe's Condor legion and the Italian fascist Aviazone Legionaria. Here was the killing of civilians and here was the lie of neutrality that shamed the British labour movement into a more pro-Republican stance. It paved the way for victory in northern Spain and eventually to the fall of Madrid on 28 March 1939. The TGWU did send some monies to aid organizations, but failed to campaign for any form of allied intervention.

'No Pasaran': Cable Street, 4 October 1936

The BUF had been growing since 1932, backed by wealthy donors and sections of the press.[25] It became more openly racist after 1935, and 'thus began the violent anti-Semitic campaign, modelled on the Nazi technique, and most notably felt in areas of London and the larger provincial towns where Jewish people congregated'.[26]

Significant sections of British ruling class did not hide their anti-Semitic tendencies as others turned a blind eye. It was fellow workers and trade unionists who took on the fascists even when protected by the police.[27] In the East End of London, the BUF grew especially among younger men and was well funded and organized. The main political parties stood by, and much of the Conservative press encouraged their antics. The Labour Party leaders told their members through the *Daily Herald* to keep away from anti-fascist activities. The BUF strongholds in Stepney and Bethnal Green were blighted areas, and the main fight was not in the streets but by campaigning on real issues that affected the local working class – slum landlords, unemployment, and ill health.

On 4 October 1936 the BUF was to march through the East End of London with thousands of supporters. The home secretary refused to ban the march, and the Jewish Board of Deputies took a 'supine attitude'. The only successful action was taken by the communists with mass propaganda and preparation so that 'The fascists shall not pass'. This was the slogan inspired by the struggle in Spain. On that day, march and counter-march were getting ready. There were 6,000 police and a mounted division – 'after the police came the fascists. They came in coaches from all parts of London and the country'. The police tried to force a path for the BUF through the anti-fascist crowd of 50,000. Some anti-fascist TGWU tram drivers abandoned their vehicles to form a road block. 'It was obvious that

25 G.C. Webber, 'Patterns of Membership and Support for the British Union of Fascists', *Journal of Contemporary History*, 1984, vol.19, no.4, pp.575–606.
26 Phil Piratin, *Our Flag Stays Red* (Lawrence & Wishart, 1948), p.16.
27 Kevin Marsh and Robert Griffiths, *Granite and Honey: The Story of Phil Piratin, Communist MP* (Manifesto Press, 2012), pp.14–28.

Figure 3: *Daily Worker*, 5 October 1936
Credit: *Daily Worker* archive at Marx Memorial Library

the fascists and the police would now turn their attention to Cable Street. We were ready [...]. Never was there such unity of all sections of the working class as was seen on the barricades at Cable Street'.[28] Orthodox Jews, Irish Catholic dockers, communists, trade unionists, women, and students fought the police while the fascists watched from behind them, and then retreated.

This show of solidarity against not just the fascists, but against an entire set of state and government forces backed by the sneering cheering press, showed what could be achieved. Such moments define an era and immediately resulted in renewed activities by a similar coalition of progressive groups demanding rights for tenants, workers, and patients.

The Indelible Stain

The moving finger writes, and having writ moves on[29]

The Spanish civil war showed the nature of internationalism more than any other event at the time, but it also exposed the depth of schisms among the left, and the historic failure to see fascism for what it truly was. Whatever approach was taken by leading figures in the labour movement there was a mass swell of opinion in favour of a united fight back. In Bristol, for example, where Stafford Cripps was a local MP, there were grass roots campaigns based around the Unity Players of the People's Theatre and linked with the Left Book Club and the NUWM struggles. While local trade unionists, communists, and socialists inside the Labour Party mounted united activities, the Labour Party leadership were opposed and sought to quell such common causes through suspensions and expulsions.[30]

Many of the strands of the struggle for a united front to oppose fascism came together through the CP's line of rank-and-file activism in the unions, against Moseley and his supporters, for the Spanish Republic, against the timid reformist leadership in the TUC and Labour Party, and for a planned progressive economy and welfare reforms. This required working with a range of supporters on committees, in the streets, and in union branches.[31]

Indeed, the CP's journal of 'political controversy' for April 1937 contained a series of articles on Spain and fascism. In his analysis of the

28 Piratin, *Our Flag*, p.23.
29 Omar Khayyám, *Rubáiyát of Omar Khayyám*, trans. Edward Fitzgerald (Bodleian Library, 2014), stanza LXXI.
30 Angela Tuckett, 'The People's Theatre in Bristol 1930–1945' (*Our History 72*, c.1978), p.9.
31 Mike Power, 'The Struggle Against Fascism and War in Britain 1931–1939' (*Our History 70, c.1977*).

fascist vote in the London County Council (LCC) elections, Pat Devine suggests that the left needed to understand working-class support for such opinions. A key element was the rejection of the United Front by Labour and unions such as the TGWU,[32] a point underlined by an account of the anti-fascist struggle in Southwark where the trades council took a leading role in the United Front but were undermined by local Labour Parties and pro-Franco union branches under Catholic influence.[33]

The move from United Front to the broader Popular Front in 1935 was based on the growing threat of fascism. A key element of this was work inside the trade unions. The left won elected positions at factory and branch level, defeated Spencerism at the Harworth strike,[34] and backed the 1936 hunger march. It was clear that during the Spanish civil war '[t]he Communist Party was the spearhead of the greatest sustained effort ever made by the people of Britain to help another country'.[35] Activists throughout the TGWU used their union positions to develop working-class unity. This solidarity-building stretched, for some, as far as the colonies.

The leadership of the TGWU were horrified by the actions of the fascists and denounced them time and time again. They understood their anti-union and anti-democratic activities, but did not appear to appreciate the ideological underpinnings. In several articles and speeches Bevin and Deakin failed to nail down the nature of fascism, and believed it would not take off in Britain due to some uniquely British characteristics. A contemporary assessment is more forensic in examining the class composition of the petit bourgeois and a 'parasitic' proletariat, unorganized in unions, and closely allied with employers. These potential fascist recruits taken together with the class collaborationism inherent in Mondism allowed fascist propaganda to reach millions. The Ulster movement was closely watched by Tory 'diehards' as a model for a fascism throughout the land.[36]

32 Pat Devine, 'Fascist Voices: An Analysis of the LCC Election Results in East London', *Discussion*, 1937, no.4, pp.19–22.

33 Dave Russell, *Southwark Trades Council 1903–1978* (Southwark Trades Council, 1978), pp.34–37.

34 Ronald Kidd, *Harworth Colliery Strike Disturbances* (NCCL, 1937).

35 Noreen Branson and Bill Moore, 'Labour-Communist Relations 1920–1951' (*Our History*, 83, 1991), p.6.

36 Raji Palme Dutt, *Fascism and Social Revolution* (Martin Lawrence, 1934), pp.236–239.

Colonialism and Racism at Work

Tacitus's life of Agricola describes his father-in-law's exploits in Britain: 'To ravage, to slaughter, to usurp under false titles, they call empire; and where they make a desert, they call it peace'.[37]

Bevin was a supporter of the Empire. His labour imperialism was the usual medley of superiority of the white man, bringing civilisation to the world, benefits to his members from preferential trade and markets, and onward Christian soldiers. He was not alone among labour movement leaders, but there was a substantial group of those fighting for an end to Empire, for national self-determination, and clear on racial equality. One persistent weakness

> lies [...] in the divisions within the movement, and above all on the corrupting influence of imperialism, especially upon certain upper sections of the workers [...] [and] their desire for an acknowledged place in existing society led to a willingness to tolerate and even defend capitalism, to turn a blind eye to and even actively support the exploitation of colonial peoples.[38]

A typical report of the time from the *Daily Worker* (19 May 1934) expressed the tensions and inequities of being a black worker in Britain.

> In Cardiff unemployed coloured seamen in the docks area are now being officially questioned in such a way as to indicate a repatriation drive. The immigration authorities are only dealing now with one race, the West Africans; this, we believe, is only the thin edge of the wedge [...].The National Union of Seamen have been agitating against coloured seamen for some time. Not very long ago the general secretary, Mr. Spence, appealed to the National Government for a stricter application of the Alien Act, and instructed their delegates boarding ships to make appeals to captains not to ship coloured seamen.

The attitude of the local unions was clear, and although the TGWU had few dealings with black workers at the time, some members did share such sentiments. The TGWU's approach to workers in the colonies is explored as a sign of the union's general ideas on race and class. While

---

37 C. Taciti (*c*.98) *De Vita Agricolae* (Clarendon Press, 1922 edition), chapter 30, p.23.
38 A.L. Morton and George Tate, *The British Labour Movement* (Lawrence & Wishart, 1956), p.298.

the British labour movement at home was fighting fascists, and seeking better deals for workers through collective bargaining, their fellow workers in the colonies remained battered and bruised in their efforts to improve their pay and conditions, establish basic civil and industrial rights, and remove their own colonialists. In such struggles the TGWU showed some awareness of common interests, provided some support, but largely failed to acknowledge the harmful presence of the British Empire.

Indian independence had gained ground across the subcontinent with support from within Britain. The 'jewel in the crown' was marching in another direction, and as disorder increased so the unease caused in the corridors of power grew. The Indian unions in the 1930s were dominated by communists, and the TUC was keen to be involved, with government support, in order to bring a more British slant to such activities.[39]

John Cliff (assistant general secretary) was particularly concerned with the situation in India. He wrote a series of articles for *The Record* in 1931 and urged the British government to grant a bigger role for the Indian unions with the enforcement of a minimum wage. The TGWU continued its commentary on the independence issue throughout the 1930s with a largely sympathetic account of the plight of Indian workers, especially in transport and in the docks. This did not fit well with the TGWU's tendency to support the Empire. They were worried about communist influence and sectarian divisions hampering what they saw as a peaceful transition to some form of self-rule.

Such views can be seen in the response to mass labour unrest throughout the West Indies over pay and conditions, union and civil rights, and against British rule. The reaction of the TGWU was instructive. Bevin himself became 'interested' in the plight of the colonies when in 1931 he was appointed to the Advisory Committee on Colonial Development – 'it was the first time Bevin came into contact with the struggling, impoverished world of the under-developed countries'.[40] In the 1930s 'the colonies, strictly so-called, were still administered autocratically from Whitehall. The West Indies were not much more than a relic from a vanished past'.[41] The TGWU was involved, and

> [t]hroughout the 1920s and the 1930s, British labor unions had sought to guide and encourage formation of West Indian affiliates. As a result, unionization was common throughout the region [...]. However, Fabian tutelage and reformist policies appeared to

39 D. Davies, 'The Politics of the TUC's Colonial Policy', *The Political Quarterly*, 1964, vol.35, no.1, pp.23–34.
40 Bullock, *Trade Union Leader*, p.435.
41 Taylor, *English History*, p.151.

have failed when workers broke out in spontaneous demonstrations throughout the region, beginning in St. Kitts in 1935 and culminating with Jamaica (and British Guiana) in 1938.[42]

This mass disaffection revealed,

> the concurrence of unrest in almost every territory in the area, the publicity given to them in the United Kingdom, the need for new lines of policy in the area to which they drew attention and the outlining of these new policies [...] were a direct consequence of these disturbances.[43]

The list of strikes and riots is a testimony to the depth of feeling of those workers involved, and the desperate plight of working-class life. Women played a crucial role at almost every level of the popular protests, especially in the planning and execution of the strikes.[44] Arthur Creech Jones – TGWU national secretary for administrative, clerical and supervisory section, elected as a Labour MP in 1935 specializing in the colonies, and later Secretary of State for the Colonies in the 1945 Labour government – wrote about the 'deplorable' social and economic conditions of the local population across the West Indies. He noted that there was 'total neglect' with terrible lives, and urged the government to grant full trade union rights and political reform within the current constitution (*The Record*, April 1940).

TGWU and State Intervention

The pattern of domestic politics remained the same, with the TGWU urging government to rearm both to confront the fascist threat and to kick-start the economy. The TGWU fought for the 40-hour week, better health and safety, and more pay rises to match increased profits. It urged the Labour Party to endorse calls for public ownership of coal and transport, and to commit to a planned economy that would banish ruinous unemployment. Again words were not matched by deeds, and the TGWU remained lukewarm on protest movements. On 5 October 1936, 207 unemployed men left Jarrow lead by Ellen Wilkinson MP with a

---

42 Sandra Meditz and Dennis Hanratty (eds), *Caribbean Islands: A Country Study* (Library of Congress, 1987) pp.37–38.

43 F.X. Mark, *Rise and Development of Labour Movements in the British Caribbean with Particular Reference to British Guyana, Jamaica and Trinidad* (PhD thesis, University of Edinburgh, 1959), p.230.

44 Richard Hart, *Labour Rebellions of the 1930s in the British Caribbean Region Colonies* (Caribbean Labour Solidarity and the Socialist History Society, 2002).

petition of 11,572 people marching to London.[45] This time there was mass support for the 300-mile march. Comrades welcomed them and arranged hospitality as they passed through, but this did not stop the Labour Party EC from condemning them. The march was a huge success and has become a touchstone of working-class protest ever since.

At the TUC's conference in 1937 further divisions arose on rearmament and lack of support for the Popular Front: 'the Labour left, spurred on by the communists, had denounced German fascism from the first day'.[46] By 1938 all had changed again. The economy was firmly on a war footing and the TUC swung behind the effort, meeting the prime minister on 23 March 1938 to agree, among other matters, to relax craft restrictions in engineering in order to facilitate greater production through more flexible working. The TGWU leadership lagged behind the militant temper of many groups, and once again unofficial action pushed the pay agenda. Such movements were condemned time and again by the TGWU leaders. At the 1937 BDC they were 'not to be tolerated', they were the work of 'disruptive groups', and worse still in some cases 'in our approach to the employers we were not helped by the series of unauthorised strikes which took place' (*The Record*, January 1938).[47]

Towards the end of 1937, the LP published *Labour's Immediate Programme*, which included a detailed plan for pensions backed by the TGWU.[48] This was the new planned and centrally funded welfare system which included a demand for a 40-hour week and for raising the school leaving age to 15 – both trade union ideas aimed at reducing the supply of labour. It also contained other important elements such as nationalization of the Bank of England, setting up a national transport board, no return to the gold standard, establishing a national industrial board, statutory holidays with pay, and more help for distressed areas. This fed into Bevin's concerns with a form of industrial democracy – the demand that trade unions be consulted by employers on every major policy with government backing. He explained to the TGWU EC that 'we all know that transport must be brought under public control and organised on an entirely new basis. I cannot see any representatives of the capitalist class agreeing to a fundamental change in the ownership of the means to life'.[49] The rub, as always, was that until that day comes, trade union leaders had to accommodate to make improvements. That was his strongest view of British labour history: compromise until salvation.

45 Tom Pickard, *Jarrow March* (Allison & Busby, 1982); Ellen Wilkinson, *The Town That Was Murdered: The Life-Story of Jarrow* (Victor Gollancz, 1939).

46 Taylor, *English History*, p.418.

47 A.F. Papworth (July 1937), 'The Biennial Conference of the TGWU' (*Labour Monthly*).

48 *Labour's Immediate Programme*, Labour Party Executive publication, 1937.

49 General Secretary quarterly report, December 1936, cited in Bullock, *Trade Union Leader*, p.599.

The TGWU's general line of argument was that, despite the fact that nearly 30 per cent of people lived in poverty, Britain was a more progressive and reformable country than before. Bevin fought for, and seemed to believe, that organized labour was being accepted as part of the national community. An example of this position was his seat on the government committee (Amulree) looking into paid holidays. Here his influence swayed the day and by 1938 over 11 million workers were covered by the scheme. Bullock notes that 'this minor social revolution appealed strongly to Bevin'.[50] He was president of the Workers' Travel Association, and in September 1937 Mr Butlin opened the first communal holiday camp in Skegness.

By 1937 the rearmament boom had greatly reduced unemployment, as Galbraith wryly noted, Hitler having eliminated unemployment in Germany proceeded to reduce it elsewhere![51] While productivity rose by 20 per cent between 1932–1937, real wages remained generally stagnant. Between 1935–1937, wages rose by 7.6 per cent while prices rose by 8.2 per cent and profits by 25 per cent. This was evidence against Citrine's argument that by co-operating with employers in production, workers would share in the benefits. Wages remained relatively low with half the working population below any acceptable national standard.

As a result, throughout 1937–1938 the wages' movement grew. Orwell had shown in *The Road to Wigan Pier* the harsh realities of workers' drudge-day lives and the attendant resentment felt by so many.[52] An increasing number of area committees were reporting improvements in wages and working conditions. There was a movement in support of mass mobilization to push up wages, especially amongst the weaker sectors. The TGWU could report great progress in the docks and waterways. By April 1937 there were negotiated pay rises for women in engineering, for beet sugar workers, and in furniture removal and warehousing. Shipbuilders and clay workers received holidays with pay, there was a guaranteed working week in flour milling, bonuses for workers at British Aluminium, and union recognition for cast stone and cast concrete workers. Elsewhere things remained bleak with 'wage slavery' in the catering trades especially associated with living-in conditions. There was an official four-month long dispute among the stable men ('lads') at Lambourn in West Berkshire over wages and union recognition (*The Record*, June 1938).

A typical example of unofficial action over pay was among over 2,000 Hull dockers. The TGWU officials urged the men back to work to allow the claim to work through the national system.[53] Another case was among the blanket workers in Witney. The four largest firms had resisted

50 Bullock, *Trade Union Leader*, p.601.
51 J.K. Galbraith, *The Age of Uncertainty* (1977), quoted from the BBC TV series.
52 George Orwell, *The Road to Wigan Pier* (Victor Gollancz, 1937).
53 *Hull Daily Mail*, 28 June 1937.

unionization until the TGWU Oxford District made a conscious effort, stemming from the CP's industrial strategy rather than TGWU centre, to recruit members and thereby win negotiating rights. Unofficial strikes remained a reality for many TGWU members despite, as the *Busman's Punch* (March 1937) warned, 'The only man who desires a strike for fun is the man who wants to go to hell for a pastime'. By their nature the extent of unofficial strikes is difficult to measure, and some are more 'unofficial' than others. Knowles agreed that 'the years 1935 to 1937, and especially 1936, were particularly notable for unofficial strikes'.[54] Indeed the situation so worried Citrine and Bevin that in 1937, the General Council of the TUC circularized trades councils to the effect that they should not actively encourage unofficial strikes.

The TGWU leaders failed to support the development of union organization in the new mass production industries with only 15 per cent density in car factories. Surveys, for example, in the London area found that most factories remained unorganized and that where there was no union presence the employers refused to pay an overtime rate for extra hours worked. In some cases, young women in particular, were not only paid very low hourly rates but had deductions taken from their pay package for items including toilet facilities. Here the reality for most workers was far from the boasts of the TGWU leadership.

The TGWU used its size and strength to become involved in a series of state-based initiatives. These included submissions to the Royal Commission in 1937 to examine geographical distribution of the industrial population.[55] Its report recommended the decentralization of industry from congested areas, indicated that the problems were of national urgency, and proposed the setting up of a central national authority, a board for industrial location responsible to the board of trade. Another example was TGWU interest in medical services, especially in industrial diseases and rehabilitation. The union was involved in the industrial health research board, plans for an NHS concerning both mental and physical health at work as with the inquiry into gastritis among London busmen. The BMA formed a joint committee with the TUC, and concerned itself with national maternity service, factories bill, and national health insurance scheme. In September 1937 TUC at Norwich announced a scientific advisory committee to link trade unions with medicine and science.

In 1937 the TGWU was the largest union with about 600,000 members (11 per cent of UK total). Bevin still dominated policy direction and was more hands-on in certain sectors, for example, flour milling through its JIC where the union gained a shorter working week but no wage increases

---

54 Knowles, *Strikes*, p.33.
55 The National Archives, Royal Commission on the Distribution of the Industrial Population, Cmd 6153 (1937–1940), known as the Barlow Report.

(*The Record*, April 1937). In the ports and tinplate industries he failed to win the pension schemes the union wanted, although he blamed the communists and rival unions rather than the employers for such failures. The union did back a local strike of Hull tug men over substantive issues of pay, hours of work, and holiday entitlements, and the question of union recognition. In September and October 1937 they struck and defeated efforts to break the strike by the use of blackleg labour.[56]

In road haulage the enforcement of standard wages and conditions through the National Joint Conciliation Board was sketchy, and Bevin this time did blame the employers and some of the workforce for conniving with the bosses. The government set up another committee of inquiry in May 1937,[57] which largely agreed with the TGWU's position and the Road Haulage Wages Act 1938 enshrined these in law.

State intervention and planning were part of the mainstream political debate. Keynes's seminal rewriting of classical economics proposed state intervention in the economy and provided an analytical, as well as social justice, basis for a welfare model that included state pensions, benefits, and health insurance. This was an important step in paving the way for the post-war settlement of nationalization of health, coal, education, and transport. British economists and political leaders had been in thrall to laissez-faire classical theories of markets. In some sense the simple notion was that they would always eventually rebalance and therefore there was no need for state intervention. This was, of course, a deliberate misreading of Adam Smith and David Ricardo amongst others,[58] but it suited the purpose of British imperial preference in trade, profit making at home, and the political dominance of capital over labour.

Keynes showed that it was possible and likely for the economy to reach equilibrium at the bottom of the trade cycle, and therefore state intervention was needed to boost demand through borrowing and higher wages and benefits (since the marginal propensity to consume was greater at lower incomes). It could be used to 'kick-start' the economy until a virtuous circle at higher levels of activity had been reached, at which point state borrowing and intervention could be reduced. This neglected Marx who argued that eventually that remedy (known to him through earlier economists recommending public works programmes) would also fail since

56 *Hull Daily Mail*, 6 and 16 October 1937.
57 Report of the Baillie Committee on the Regulation of Wages and Conditions of Service in the Road Transport Industry (Goods), 3 November 1937, Cmd 5440; Modern Records Centre MSS.292/712.5/1/261–263.
58 Adam Smith (1723–1790) and David Ricardo (1772–1823) were classical economists; the former developed the notion that a free-market economy is self-organizing, and the latter developed the theory of rent as a surplus payment to a factor over and above what was necessary to keep it in its present use.

the contradictions of the capitalist system would always result in crises.[59] It also ignored, although at the same time sought to contradict, the efforts by the USSR with its longer term state planning and state ownership.[60] While the debate raged at the time it did not really become part of the public domain of national politics until 1944, with the end of the war in sight and welfare reforms at the top of the agenda along with reconstruction. The New Deal in America had of course followed a similar policy but with a more pragmatic and a less ideological twist.[61]

This conversion happened by necessity rather than by informed policy making:

> Great Britain, as a result of the changes made since 1929, has departed a long distance from the almost entirely planless economy of the years before the slump. She possesses today a managed currency, a largely managed foreign trade, a considerably managed system of agricultural production, and a managed system of industrial production extending to coal and steel.[62]

These were increasingly joined by a partly managed housebuilding policy, a grid under the Central Electricity Board, the formation of the London Passenger Transport Board, and the development of trading estates in derelict areas. This was real state intervention in the economy, but was not economic planning as such. Despite this embedding of the TGWU leadership inside the framework of industrial relations, the mood in the regions was still one of stark amazement that in a country teeming with wealth, millions were on the breadline. The frustration of many local leaders was heartfelt: 'what a pity the workers as a whole tolerate such a system when the remedy is in their own hands. What a tragedy they are so little interested in their own welfare and salvation'.[63]

TGWU Education in the 1930s

TGWU educational development took off in 1937. Before that 'its practical support for its members taking part in these activities was woefully inadequate for the size of the organisation and for its strategic role in the

59 Karl Marx (1849) *Wage Labour and Capital* (Progress Publishers, Selected Works, 1969 edition), pp.142–174.
60 Maurice Dobb, *Russian Economic Development Since the Revolution* (Routledge, 2012).
61 Arthur Schlesinger, *The Coming of the New Deal: The Age of Roosevelt, 1933–1935* (Houghton Mifflin Harcourt, 2003).
62 G.D.H. Cole, *Practical Economics* (Penguin, 1937), p.242.
63 Tyne and Wear Area Committee minutes, 22 April 1936.

new mass-production and transport industries'. As a result of this official inertia there was a grass roots movement within the union to develop education in parallel with the rank-and-file movement. 'It was to fill this gap, as well as to counter the influence of the Left, that the leadership supported a radical extension to the education programme at the end of the 1930s, which changed its character and orientation for the rest of the century'.[64] Women's education was becoming increasingly important as more joined. Specialist women's education came later, but by 1933 TUC weekend courses were being supported by the TGWU. The union even sponsored a leading member, Sister Durkin, to attend a summer school in the USA in 1939.

The communists had always put education of members and followers at the heart of their campaigns. Knowledge of history mattered, but it was the link of political economy with everyday workers' struggle, and then with the necessity for a socialist revolution that was at the centre of the CP's case. The motivation for such work was clear. Communists felt that history was on their side after the 1917 Russian Revolution, and that a knowledge of class struggle would inform and encourage such struggles today; that education was in and of itself a benefit to individuals and the cause; and that it helped shine a light on the inadequacy of right-wing social democracy and thereby win over union activists.

The penny had dropped for the TGWU leadership and they now entered into union education with more enthusiasm in order to see off the dangerous communists and to restore credibility to their own more collaborative industrial strategies. Fisher refers to these years (1937–1939) as the 'Great Leap Forward'. It was Bevin's concern to combat communist influence that made him look again at the TGWU's education provision. The partial economic upturn after 1935 meant renewed growth for the union, and this brought in both younger workers and more women unencumbered by memories of the 1920s. Whatever Bevin himself thought, it was key officials that pushed for more education. Harold Clay, Arthur Creech Jones, and John Price all fought for extra funds and were enthusiastically backed by area and regional leaders.[65]

The turning point seems to have come at the 1935 BDC. A motion from the Central London Taxicabs, a communist stronghold, wanted a national education scheme linked with the National Council of Labour Colleges (NCLC) for all members with a free correspondence course.[66] The NCLC was seen as a communist body and its supporters argued that

64 John Fisher, *Bread on the Waters: A History of TGWU Education 1922–2000* (Lawrence & Wishart, 2005), pp.39–41.
65 John Holford, 'Britain's Forgotten Minister of Adult Education: Arthur Creech Jones and a Socialist Strategy for Development and Democracy in Africa', *Proceedings of the 36th Adult Education Conference*, 1995, pp.71–76, Alberta, Canada.
66 Fisher, *Bread on the Waters*, p.48.

its education was for the working class and in favour of class struggle. Bevin blocked this route, but it forced him to face up to the needs for educational expenditure and the development of TGWU courses. He wrote in *The Record* (February 1937) that the union must launch its own educational programme to fight for the centre ground politically and for collaborative progress industrially. His initial idea was to provide a fairly narrow set of courses focusing on the union itself, and avoiding the fertile ground for communists of the wider economic and political systems. At the 1937 BDC he paved the way both for the type of courses he wanted and for the man to lead the education programme, John Price.[67]

He was one of Bevin's 'young men', an anti-communist docker with a strong sense of trade unionism. He launched the programme, 'The Union: Its Work and Problems', which was topped up by day and weekend schools at district level. The course was to be a *vademecum* for union activists and funded by increasing membership and lack of strike action. A key desire was to assert total union control over all education both inside the union and with outside bodies such as the Workers' Educational Association (WEA) and NCLC. This was part of the need to keep a rigid hierarchical union structure to maintain the integrity of the vast sprawling mass of union activities. The importance of fighting the communists in the field of education had become more urgent with the founding in 1933 of the Marx Memorial Library as a resource for adult cadres.[68]

In 1938 the new course was developed mainly by John Price and Ellen McCullough. They were assisted by national secretaries and Bevin kept a watchful eye on its contents. It would appear that he wanted to steer the entire enterprise away from any 'leftist' contamination from his removal of the section on workers' control. By 1939 the union's top-heavy decision-making systems finally came around to approving the roll out of the correspondence course. The course itself was unexceptional: background to the union; union structure; union functions; how to improve terms and conditions for members; bargaining machinery; and a special section on women and young workers. The course was delivered in a series of booklets with bibliography and study notes. It was hard going with undigested facts being the main diet, and tough standards to achieve the sought-after certificate. In May 1939 Bevin made this statement in his GS report: 'I regard this publication as one of the best things we have done in the union, and I would ask, therefore, that you make it a special feature in your report to the area committees, and also in any address given to branches'.[69]

67 Tony Topham, 'Education Policy in the TGWU, 1922–1944: A Tribute to John Price', *The Industrial Tutor*, vol.5, no.5, pp.51–52.
68 Andrew Rothstein, *A House on Clerkenwell Green* (MML, 1983), p.75.
69 General Secretary quarterly report, May 1939, cited in Fisher, *Bread on the Waters*, p.59.

The TGWU leadership at national and area level pushed the education message, and alongside started to publish a series of articles on the role of various union officers including branch secretary and chairman. In the late 1930s Bevin's health was indifferent and Deakin began to exercise more influence over union direction. This included his strong belief in effective administration, and the need to 'professionalize' the union from top to bottom. This gave further impetus to both the educational courses and the use of 'hints' on office holding.

Just before the war engulfed these initiatives, the TGWU set up its own education committee. It started work on 3 May 1939 and was clearly meant to fight for Bevin's vision of the so-called 'centre ground' inside the union and the wider labour movement. 'One of Price's first duties was to prepare an education scheme which would train officers and lay members of the Union in the wide range of legal and economic as well as industrial questions with which they had now to be acquainted'.[70]

Busmen Again: Provincial and Metropolitan

There was progress in organizing the provincial bus industry as three large companies started to dominate through the purchase of smaller older firms. They used their market power to impose harsher conditions on the staff, and this generated several unofficial strikes in 1936 and 1937. Bevin saw such disputes as counter-productive, and that the movement towards national bargaining came not from the employers, but from 'a combination of rank-and-file militancy and some canny leadership by union officials'.[71]

Bevin was largely unimpressed and not that interested in the workers of the privately owned provincial bus companies. He saw them as difficult to organize, lacking union discipline, and prone to wildcat strikes. In Hull, for example, there was a strike by the bus workers in some parts of the city over the refusal of the employers to meet with the union men.[72]

While most had become members of the TGWU, some joined the National Union of Railwaymen. This multi-unionism was not a handicap, but the divided and incoherent employers were. The busmen worked long hours, sometimes an 11-hour shift. Conductors were paid less than drivers, and for most of the 1930s there were no paid holidays. In contrast the London busmen had developed a communist-led rank-and-file organization that was able to push up wages and improve other terms and conditions. Despite this clear example of the benefits of unionization, many provincial drivers were reluctant to join up. One reason was that

70 Bullock, *Trade Union Leader*, pp.621–622.
71 Temple, '"A Difficult and Peculiar Section"', p.198.
72 *Hull Daily Mail*, 4 May 1937.

[p]rovincial bus workers were scattered throughout the country, they were divided between many employers, and some of them were based in relatively inaccessible depots. It was therefore much harder to organize them than it was to recruit London bus workers into the union. It is also reasonable to assume that geographical isolation made it more difficult for union officials to maintain discipline over provincial bus workers.[73]

In Wilts and Dorset, for example, trade unionism was generally limited and this sense of isolation from the wider working-class movement spilled over into the consciousness of the bus workers. The use of casual staff by the companies also mitigated against unionization. Nonetheless, the example of the London busmen did seep through and more militant elements in the provinces fought for a 100 per cent membership and branch control over shop stewards. Indeed, some of the London activists toured the provinces in a recruitment drive. As a result, by 1938 it is estimated that about two-fifths of the 150,000 passenger services workers in the TGWU were based in provincial bus companies. The TGWU used the well tried and tested formulation of 'coercive comparison' to negotiate terms and conditions for provincial busmen based on those of municipal bus staff. Temple notes, however, that

> Ernest Bevin blamed unofficial industrial action by 600 busmen in Northampton, who struck for two weeks in January 1936, for undermining hopes of persuading provincial bus employers to join the NJIC [...]. Within weeks, however, serious unofficial industrial action had broken out. Around 10,000 workers employed by Scottish Motor Traction and its subsidiaries went on strike over pay and conditions in March. In the following month, approximately 5,000 provincial busmen in the TGWU walked out over pay and conditions in Kent, Oxford, Northampton, East Yorkshire, and the Eastern counties. Busmen also voted to strike in Dudley. The strikes petered out quickly but not before more damage had been done to the unions' case for national negotiations.[74]

The 1937 'Coronation' Bus Strike

In December 1936 the London busmen started negotiations on improved pay and conditions including for a seven-and-a-half-hour working day. Their core demands were rejected and the union, with Bevin's backing,

---

73 Temple, "'A Difficult and Peculiar Section'", p.201.
74 Temple, "'A Difficult and Peculiar Section'", pp.204–205.

kept negotiating. The GEC accepted the busmen's overwhelming vote to strike after negotiations failed. Throughout April and May the rank-and-file leaders were negotiating and organizing the strike, but Bevin, while publicly in support, was seeking a deal behind the backs of the members.

The rank-and-file leaders controlled the union's Central London Bus Committee and their leader Bert Papworth was elected to the GEC. They began to negotiate through the constitutional route, and after six months of talks the new contract was due to start in February 1937. The transport board held firm and refused to cut hours. The men were unhappy – traffic had increased, the speed limit had been raised to 30 mph, there were bigger buses to drive, and they had to pick up passengers when hailed as there were no fixed stops.

Papworth (*Daily Worker*, 24 April 1937) repudiated popular sentiments that communists had deliberately called the strike during the Coronation:

> Are men extremists who have tried to get their conditions altered, and have gone through every avenue of constitutional machinery open to them? [...] It is not our fault that the date of the crisis falls near to Coronation period. Kings have come and gone since the talks began. We did not fix the date of the Coronation, nor do we spoil for a strike. We want a settlement.

The employers still insisted on a strict timetable which meant crews had to turn around with no breaks. Hours of duty changed on a daily basis as timetables become more complex and random. Irregular meal times and the stress of worsening conditions were blamed on the high levels of gastric problems among the men. After further negotiations the union called an official strike from 30 April 1937. London was busier than usual as the coronation of George VI was due on 12 May. Bevin wanted the strike postponed for further negotiations, but it went ahead. On 1 May all 26,000 men came out.

The next day the Ministry of Labour appointed a court of inquiry (under the 1919 Industrial Courts Act). Bevin made the case for the men (*The Record*, May 1937). Its findings reported on 6 May partially supported the union case. The board of transport now agreed to consider the men's demands through a joint body with the union, but promised nothing. On 8 May 1937 intensive efforts were made, through the medium of the Minister of Labour, to secure a return to work on the basis of vague half-promises contained in the report. Papworth denounced the whole inquiry as a 'heads I win – tails you lose' affair (*Daily Worker*, 8 May 1937).

Bevin and the TGWU advised the men to return to work. The rank-and-file Central Bus Committee urged rejection of the deal and repudiated the GEC's advice. In Bert Papworth's own stronghold at Chelverton Road, the vote was 374 to 3 to continue the strike.[75]

The militants won and urged the tram and trolley men to join them on strike. This ploy failed, with Bevin firmly against involving other groups. Despite fierce propaganda activity and pickets the strikers could not bring out the others in solidarity. On the fourth week of the strike, on 26 May Bevin persuaded the GEC to revoke the grant of plenary powers to the Central Bus Committee and secured a return to work (with no victimization) on the terms rejected earlier. On 28 May the strike ended after one month. They did not win a shorter working day and the TGWU GEC ordered them back to work despite votes by the men to stay on strike.

As a result of this showdown with the London busmen, Bevin asked the GEC for more powers to curb unofficial action. The GEC suspended the busmen's machinery. Over the summer of 1937, the TGWU began to discipline activists associated with the strike. The *Daily Worker* (4 September) now revealed 'yet another expulsion' ordered by the union. The victim this time was Emile Burns who had 'incurred the wrath of the mandarins of Transport House'. The EC stood accused of 'suspension of union machinery, conclusion of new agreements, abolition of committees, expulsion and suspensions'. Red scare tactics were now employed, 'the Communist Party showed much interest in these unofficial strikes [...] and a Communist document, analysing the mistakes made by Party members in the Scottish strike and the lessons to be learned for the intensification of Party activity in the bus industry, fell into Bevin's hands'.[76] Bevin reported this document to a meeting of the GEC. It read:

All comrades should realise that the TGWU is now the spearhead in this country of the drive against working-class unity. Bevin's power depends on his position in his own union. A decisive change in the TGWU would result in the establishment of the United Front in this country. The whole Party thus has a special responsibility for work amongst this section of workers.[77]

Bevin now took his revenge.[78]

On 4 June the GEC suspended the special constitution of the Central Bus Section and ordered an inquiry into its conduct – a witch-hunt by

75 Fuller, *Radical Aristocrats*, p.151.
76 Bullock, *Trade Union Leader*, pp.606–607.
77 Bullock, *Trade Union Leader*, pp.606–607.
78 Fuller, *Radical Aristocrats*, pp.149–159.

any other name. It lasted ten days, with Deakin as secretary, and their recommendations were presented to the TGWU BDC in Torquay in July. The delegates held a secret session over the role of 'unofficial movements' in the bus strike. Deakin was the main prosecutor, attacking the role of the CP and pushing for sanctions against the leaders.

The upshot, as Bevin and Deakin had planned all along, was to declare the Rank-and-File Movement 'subversive', and to expel its leaders, Papworth, Payne, and Jones. Bevin introduced new rules to strengthen the union's ability to expel dissident members. Most busmen stayed inside the TGWU and the CP supported their 'stay and fight' position. A few did form a breakaway union, the National Passenger Workers' Union. Papworth and Jones soon returned to the fold and both were elected onto the GEC.

The London bus workers' group was without a doubt the 'most effective of the "rank-and-file" movements initiated by the CP. As we have seen the irony was that it was Bevin's own decision to accept wage cuts in 1932 that allowed militancy to grow and the communists to develop their formidable organisation among the busmen'.[79] While busmen's wages were always the centre of the cause, they sought to widen their appeal with links to tramway men and provincial bus workers, and deepen it with anti-fascist activities at home and sponsoring aid to the Spanish Republic.

The *Busman's Punch* (No 34 August 1935) had earlier defended its role:

This movement stands for 100 per cent membership of the T&GW union. It does not stand for breakaways of any kind. This movement stands for the right of using the strike weapon. It does not stand for the indiscriminate use of that weapon. This movement hopes to see the supporters of its policy gain representative positions. It is not an electoral machine; nor does it exist for the purpose of glorifying individuals.

It was the so-called Coronation strike in 1937 that allowed Bevin to fight for the unity he craved and the ending of the unofficial action he hated. This search for constitutionality within the TGWU allowed a limit on participatory democracy and enhanced the national leadership, but did so at the cost of fuelling both indifference and opposition among the membership.[80]

79 Branson, *Communist Party*, p.93.
80 Allen, *Trade Union Leadership*, pp.63–73.

The TGWU on the Brink of War

In 1937, TGWU membership was 654,510. Area No. 1, London and the South East, alone had 183,000 members. Income for that year was £931,091 with a general fund of £908,000. Six of the nine trade groups were major unions in their own right – Docks (87,509); Waterways (8,000); Road Passenger Transport (150,836); Road Commercial Transport (79,991); General Workers (171,000); Building Trades (32,422); Metal, Engineering and Chemical (96,037); Administrative, Clerical and Supervisory (9,214); and Power Workers (28,709). There were separate national groups inside the General Workers such as for agriculture, government and local government, and flour milling. A further national section for fishermen was started up after the amalgamation of the Scottish Fisherman's Union and the Humber Trawlermen's Union, and the TGWU helped secure the 1938 Sea Fish Industry Act.

Area committees were generally reporting that their members were 'very well employed' by 1938. Union officials were busy with negotiating wage increases and improved conditions. New groups were being formed in areas adjacent to larger union groups, but dock workers and those others on the waterways still struggled to catch up. In some cases the threat of strikes hastened the improvements as with some brick works, and where there was some worsening in trade in late 1938, the slack was picked up in the growth in armaments and related businesses.

The TGWU leaders believed that 'by 1938 they [unions] had become an essential part of the industrial structure of the country'.[81] There was, therefore, the need for a new breed of union officer working within a changed union organizational system. This new generation of trade union leaders had to negotiate using better quality information when dealing with management, on JICs, before a tribunal, or as delegates to conferences. The TGWU developed an Information and Statistics Department and in 1937 this merged with the Political and International Department, under John Price. As the state intervened more in industrial life, so trade union officials dealt more readily with government officials. It was preparation for war that accelerated this process as government interventions grew.

The TGWU was fully behind rearmament and defence growth to ward off the threat from German Nazis. The unions were co-opted to help put industrial activity onto a war footing, such as building 12,000 new planes. The TUC, with Citrine and Bevin in charge, met the prime minister and expressed their concerns about his policy of appeasement, on Spain, and with the Anglo-Italian agreement. They also noted the huge profits being made from rearmament.

---

81 Bullock, *Trade Union Leader*, p.621.

Paradoxically, Bevin's formal regulatory approach was helped, not as he sometimes argued, hindered by strike action, both official and unofficial. In September and November 1937 there were strikes in Area 1 at Bouts-Tillotson and Carter Patterson. Drivers at Smithfield meat market in London quickly organized and pressed for changes in the 'accumulative week'. In October 1937 200 hundred drivers took unofficial strike action over the summary dismissal of a washer. They were joined by porters and thereby paralyzed the work of Smithfield meat market forcing a climb down by the employers.

In 1938, with some sections of the economy booming under rearmament and government intervention, the RTC group were able to push for further improvements. The Road Haulage Wages Act (1938) had boosted membership to about 80,000, but final national agreements were still hard to achieve given employer hostility. The first statutory order came in January 1940. The pay deal gave unorganized workers a 'fair' pay rise, and in March 1940 the pay of organized workers was also uplifted. The TGWU was pleased with the initial improvements but decried the lack of greater recruitment despite the successful work of the union. Such corporatist arrangements favoured by Bevin took away from the trade union some of its basic powers of persuasion, but the Mondist response was that this was a better deal than any achievable in the current situation through traditional trade union 'stand and deliver' tactics.

Bevin knew full well that the larger employers alongside the Ministry of Labour favoured tripartite agreements. Dock work was hard and conditions dangerous. The dominant issue remained the nature and form of 'casualization'. In June 1938 the TGWU dock group ramped up pressure on employers. 'Under the threat of war the employers became more responsive and four days later the National Joint Council for Dock Labour was agreed'.[82] As an example of both the politicization of workers and the desperate failure of the labour movement leadership on fascist aggression, the Southampton dockers refused to unload Japanese goods from the Duchess of Richmond which was docked in Southampton in 1937. Three leading communist dockers were sacked with the connivance of the TGWU officials who then prevented a strike by other workers to win reinstatement for those victimized.[83] Teesside dockers also refused to load iron for Japan as part of a wider unofficial embargo which extended to the dockers of Liverpool, Glasgow, and Le Havre.

On the bigger stage, appeasement reached its apogee of fear as Chamberlain sought to stave off the Nazi war machine through the landmark meeting in Munich. The Munich agreement between Germany, Italy, France, and the UK of 30 September 1938 was deemed to be a

82 Allen, *Trade Union Leadership*, p.174.
83 Details provided by Adrian Weir.

craven retreat by liberal democracies in the face of fascist and Nazi threats. All that came from this act of shameful submission and the invasion of Czechoslovakia was more rearmament. The British government and its supporters were ill-prepared for war, were indifferent to the fate of others, and incapable of uniting the country against the fascist threat. At the same time the Popular Front grew ever more popular. 'The Munich agreement of 1938 perfectly demonstrated this combination of confident aggression on one side, fear and concession on the other, which is why for generations the very word "Munich" became a synonym [...] for craven retreat'.[84]

Before war was formally declared on 1 September 1939, the trade unions went about their business in an atmosphere of carrying on and yet waiting and watching for doomsday. Even at the Labour Party conference in Southport in 1939, Bevin – still officially representing the TGWU – opposed the Popular Front. In the winter of 1938–1939 Bevin was in charge of preparing docks, road haulage, demolition, milling and provender for war. In July 1939 he persuaded the JICs for flour milling and provender to set up a civilian defence committee which operated through 15 area committees with provision for air raids, labour pooling, and the supply of flour and feeding stuffs in an emergency. He was a member of the Port and Transit Committee and Constructional Committee. He was in charge through the TGWU of moving dockers from east to west coast ports and agreeing the National Joint Council for Dock Labour. The principle was one of civilian employment during war, and this enabled the union to be involved with pay and conditions issues. In December 1938 the TUC agreed to join the National Services Committee with conscription through the Military Service Act.

In July 1939 the TGWU BDC saw Bevin as general secretary for the last time. He formally relinquished office in March 1946.

Part I has discussed the TGWU's path from the election of the national government in 1931 to the start of war in 1939. The TGWU was larger, more centralized, and its leaders were listened to and consulted with by large employers and state bodies. Under this successful surface ran deep unresolved issues on pay, job security, workers' rights, equality, and conditions of employment. National bargaining systems had removed many of the worst practices, but had not ended the blight of working-class lives,

> apart from Messrs Rolls Royce employment is not good, the Textile Trades are very bad – many members having been dismissed from the Celanese Works, while the whole of the Lace Workers have been unemployed or are working very short time. The Building

84 Hobsbawm, *Age of Extremes*, p.146.

Trade being slowed down, many men have been dismissed from the Railway Works.[85]

Activists and shop stewards were still victimized, and Bevin's hostility to the left in the union was unabated. As soon as war arrived this changed, as demand for war goods and services soared, employment grew, large numbers of women joined the workforce and the TGWU, and thus the TGWU changed into a wartime union.

Andrew Murray argues that '[t]he union's undoubted achievements, and the benefits that working people gained from them in the very difficult decade of the 1930s, should not blind us to the faults of the T&G at the time'.[86] These 'faults' included Bevin's intolerant authoritarian leadership as seen in the treatment of the London busmen's leaders; his support for Empire; his leaning towards class collaboration rather than class struggle as witnessed in his opposition to all unofficial action against employers; and despite his strong anti-fascism and decisive calls for rearmament, his reluctance to support the Spanish Republic and the anti-fascists at home with action.

Part I: Questions for Discussion

- How did unemployment undermine national bargaining?
- Why were some workers attracted by fascism?
- What were the main consequences for the TGWU of its leaders' anti-communism?

---

85 Midlands District Council minutes, 1938, cited by Stevenson.
86 Andrew Murray, The T & G Story (Lawrence & Wishart, 2008), p.71.

II

War and Welfare, 1939–1945

Introduction

The war was the shattering climax of years of increased nationalism, belligerent expansionist ideologies, and the fraught economic and social perils of unemployment. Throughout the 1930s Japan, Italy, and Germany invaded other countries and glorified in their aggressive wars. In the British labour movement, there were bitter arguments about how best to avoid war and then how best to prepare for one.

The devastation of the war years was seen in the unknown final death toll as millions of civilians were murdered without scruple and without an abacus for the fallen.

The price of defeat by the German National Socialist regime, as demonstrated in Poland and the occupied parts of the USSR, and by the fate of the Jews, whose systematic extermination gradually became known to an incredulous world, was enslavement and death. Hence the war was waged without limit. The Second World War escalated mass war into total war.[1]

This volume of the history of the TGWU cannot recount the numerous traumatic events of the war, nor list the heroic acts on the battlefield, in the forests of resistance, in factories and mines, and at home. The emphasis will be on developments within the union with a focus on wartime collective bargaining, wage policies, and labour mobilization. The commitment of the union leaders and members to the war effort was total, but so was their determination to avoid being the cannon fodder for capitalist profit making.

The war, when it came, was more in keeping with nineteenth-century ideals of progress and reaction. Churchill was an imperialist anti-communist and de Gaulle was a reactionary Catholic, but both were anti-Hitler.

---

1 Hobsbawm, *Age of Extremes*, p.43.

For the Second World War was, for those on the winning side, not merely a struggle for military victory, but – even in Britain and the USA – for a better society [...]. A British government under Winston Churchill committed itself, in the midst of a desperate war, to a comprehensive welfare state and full employment.[2]

In June 1941 Germany invaded the USSR (Operation Barbarossa) and the USA entered (after the Japanese attack on Pearl Harbour in December) to make it a world war. By 1943 the Allies were winning, and at home economic life was in full war mode. Thoughts were turning to the post-war settlement. The real post-war world in Europe and South East Asia was being forged by the Resistance movements rather than by the great leaders, and it was mainly such fighters who formed post-war governments. Reactionary Catholics, the wealthy, nativists, and others who had backed the fascists were forced onto the back foot. The improvements to working-class life after the war were a step-change in modern historical terms, but were fought for and fought over inside the TGWU and the wider labour movement.

The Second World War had a profound effect on the trade union and working-class movement. In the workplaces and at all levels of national life the unions played a key role in the successful fight against fascism. In 1940 Winston Churchill formed a coalition government ousting the Tory government under Chamberlain. He realized the importance of winning the support of the unions in any national effort, and so he took the unusual step of bringing Ernest Bevin into the government as Minister of Labour. Arthur Deakin became acting general secretary of the TGWU during the war years. Mass mobilization of troops meant labour shortages, and these were met by the influx of new workers into industry which boosted trade union membership, and as a result, the TGWU passed the one million mark in 1942. Many women joined the workforce and the TGWU fought, and in some cases won, equal pay for equal work.

The role of the state was a central aspect of both the ideological struggle and the realities of political differences. The classic Marxist argument is that all the elements of the state apparatus – Parliament, police, judiciary, military, secret service, civil service – are the instruments of class rule. In contrast the dominant liberal democracy case, pursued by the TGWU leaders, is that the state is neutral as between classes, and that its role is to make the rules, ensure everyone obeys the rules, and that the rules coincide with the national interest. This matters since it directly impinges on trade union policy towards collective bargaining, strikes, and arbitration. Sassoon notes in his panoramic view of European socialism, 'It is not unsurprising that, in spite of the wealth of left thinking in the 1930s

2 Hobsbawm, *Age of Extremes*, p.161.

on planning and social reorganization, there was a conspicuous silence on reorganization of the state'.[3] As the clear and present danger of invasion and defeat receded towards the end of 1943 so workers looked forward to 'a brave new world'.

The number of strikes rose dramatically as union activists pushed back against wage restraint, and this tide of militancy fed into the wider debates about a planned economy, a larger state sector, more just distribution of worldly goods, and the movement for comprehensive health, welfare, and education. The TGWU played its part in formulating some of these policies, but was split politically as anti-communist rhetoric dampened and weakened the stronger socialist calls for nationalization, greater democracy, and equality.

The government became the main customer for industrial production during the war with over 1.6 million workers employed in state-owned factories. This went hand in hand with greater state regulation of the private sector.

'The creation of a total war economy also transformed the lives of workers: their wages, working conditions, and the time spent at their jobs'.[4] For many the working day was long, they were away from home, and there was an influx of new workers, especially women. All this added up to full employment, and towns such as Oxford, Coventry, and London grew rapidly. Even the previously ravaged regions of Scotland, South Wales, and the North East prospered. A picture developed of greater class consciousness that became 'superimposed upon older loyalties'.[5]

3 Donald Sassoon, *One Hundred Years of Socialism: The West European Left in the Twentieth Century* (Fontana, 1996), p.58; Clement Attlee, *The Labour Party in Perspective* (Victor Gollancz, 1937).

4 Geoffrey Field, *Blood, Sweat, and Toil: Remaking the British Working Class, 1939–1945* (Oxford University Press, 2011), p.80.

5 Field, *Blood, Sweat, and Toil*, p.80.

4

1939–1942: The European War

Introduction

This chapter examines the start of war, and the creation of a coalition government under Churchill with Bevin as Minister of Labour. This meant a major role for the unions in the war economy, and they formally endorsed both industrial conscription and the banning of strikes through Order 1305. Nonetheless, the TGWU maintained the need for voluntary collective bargaining, and sought to control militants through sustained anti-communism and improved administration and education. This all changed with the Nazi invasion of the USSR when the communists were welcomed into the fold for the duration. Meanwhile the realities in workplaces did not match the rhetoric of the union's powerful national presence.

With the collapse of Czechoslovakia on 15 March 1939 came the realization that Hitler had made fools and worse of the national government. Over the summer the government failed to secure an alliance with the USSR, failed to convince Hitler that they would actually fight, but also failed to appease him.

The Start of War and the 'Battle of Britain'

On 1 September 1939 war was declared. The so-called 'phoney war' allowed for the distribution of gas masks, organization of the black out, and the evacuation of London, but 'these troubles fell upon those least able to cope with them. The poor housed the poor. The wealthier classes [...] evaded their responsibilities throughout the war'.[1]

This government of appeasers did very little to put the country on a war footing, and they remained a national government in name only. The

---

1 Taylor, *English History*, p.455.

Tories dithered with fantasies of weak opponents even as U-boats were sinking merchant ships. By early 1940 with the Soviet invasion of Finland the government remained blind to events, and in April Chamberlain still argued that Hitler had 'missed the bus'. By early May, after much fuss, Chamberlain resigned and was replaced by the flawed but able Churchill.

Churchill's coalition government was mainly old guard Conservatives plus a few Labour members including Attlee. The two main outsiders brought into Cabinet were Beaverbrook as Minister of Aircraft Production but really Churchill's main adviser, and Bevin as Minister of Labour. This appointment was welcomed throughout the TGWU with the slogan 'Ernie'll sort it out'. On 22 May 1940 the Emergency Powers Act gave government unlimited powers over citizens.

On the industrial front, there was a general reluctance to pursue a national wages' policy as government preferred voluntary arrangements between unions and employers. Prices rose in late 1939 and the chancellor (John Simon) called a meeting of the National Joint Advisory Committee on 6 December 1939 on the wage-price spiral. He urged wage restraint. The emergency budget in September 1939 had already raised taxes, but it gave the impression that 'the Government was as dangerously muddled and complacent in its approach to economic affairs as it appeared to be in its organization of military activities'.[2] Keynes provided a more coherent analysis with solutions: control of wages, savings, taxation, rationing, and prices to limit consumption of normal goods and services as resources were diverted to the war economy.[3] Keynes wanted trade union support in control of wages through a series of policies – 'deferred income scheme' – which became post-war credits.

The unions were deeply suspicious of the Chamberlain government, and Bevin made his position clear in *The Record* in October 1939 that unions would only join government committees as equals and not as an act of patronage. The TUC refused to stop wage claims but also agreed to be responsible. Once the war was underway Bevin sought the means to remove wages from controversy through a national arbitration tribunal with its legally binding Order 1305 to stop strikes and lockouts.

Trade unions affiliated to the TUC increased their membership during the war from roughly four and a half million to around seven-and-a-half million. This was accompanied by the spread of recognition agreements in industries in which unions had only a toe-hold before the war. Many unions had to rapidly alter their rules to allow those members called up to the armed forces to keep their union cards. This extension of trade union rights was underwritten by the government who denied war contracts

2 Roberts, *National Wages Policy*, p.27.

3 J.M. Keynes, *How to Pay for the War: A Radical Plan for the Chancellor of the Exchequer* (MacMillan, 1940).

to firms (under the Essential Works Order) who failed to conform to minimum standards demanded by the unions.

An important aspect of the start of war for many industrial workers was the sense of both being involved in a just war against fascism, and also being part of a war effort not well co-ordinated by employers and government. With war came a renewed urgency for both productivity and trade unionism. One personal account captures the forces at play:

> The real change at Radiators, so far as trade unionism was concerned, came with the war. First, we had this large group of workers coming down from Wolverton – very trade-union minded and earning higher rates than us. Then there was the effect of women workers and of the Emergency Works order.[4]

The confidence of trade unions grew, for instance, the TGWU in Coventry led the demand for JPCs. This established the principle of consultative rights on matters relating to planning and organizing production for workers, and over 4,500 such committees were established in the engineering and aircraft industries, ordnance factories, and dockyards. They laid the basis for the trade unions' role over the next 40 years, until the Thatcher governments of the 1980s unravelled the post-war settlement to the detriment of the working class as a whole.

At the start of the war the TUC and the TGWU demanded full participation in decisions from the government. Representatives from the TUC were placed on most relevant committees. This meant sitting down with big business on joint consultative committees, and agreeing an industrial and political truce. This demobilization of the movement resulted in a slack period for TGWU branches and their usual activities. There was outrageous profiteering and mismanagement in the war effort. In 1940 most workers saw a reduction in the living standards and even in Coventry, the heart of the munitions industry, only about half of families saw any improvements.

A TGWU statement 'war and the workers' poignantly summarized the situation: 'war is not only a great tragedy for the workers, who have to make the greatest sacrifices and bear the heaviest burdens, but, while it lasts, it is a period of great danger to their liberties and hard-won standards'. Bevin explained: 'our task in war time is to keep in touch with members called up; to prevent profiteering and a rise in food prices; and we need to be involved in the running of the docks' (*The Record*, October 1939). This matched the STUC manifesto in which the workers of Scotland were urged to fight the Nazis.

---

4 Arthur Excell, *The Politics of the Production Line: Autobiography of an Oxford Car Worker* (History Workshop Journal, 1981), p.53.

The TGWU's main message was that the union was carrying out its 'business as usual' with protection for dockers involved in the transfer schemes; fighting for equal pay for women; trying to sort out transport problems caused by the black out; and making sure wages kept up with prices. These aims required constant vigilance in dealings with government departments to ensure employers did not ignore health and safety issues as much work became harder and more stressful. It also involved, early in 1940, negotiating pay rises for a range of union members linked with war bonuses in sectors such as cement, and the soap and candle trades.

In May and June 1940 the start of the war proper was a disaster. Hitler overran Belgium and Holland, and on 27 May the Dunkirk evacuation started. On 22 June, Petain signed an armistice with Germany, and France was lost. By July Churchill issued his war aims – total victory or unconditional surrender to back up earlier statements of victory at all costs. The 'finest hour' had now arrived and by mid-June 1940 a German invasion was imminent. German nationals and fascists were interned including Mosely and his wife. Churchill started the push to win over Roosevelt and the Americans. Meanwhile, the TWGU backed the Labour Party's agreement for an electoral truce and the postponement of the general election.

On 16 July 1940 Hitler ordered the invasion of the British Isles and thus began the 'Battle of Britain' with the full attack starting on 13 August. By 15 September the British had won the air war and the invasion never happened. At this juncture the war was between Britain and Germany and had become one of attrition including withstanding the 'blitz' from September to November 1940. Thus 1940 ended with the threat of invasion lifted but with fighting on all fronts intensifying.

At home the major concern was supply of war materials, logistics of delivery, and the control and maintenance of life under war conditions. The Battle of the Atlantic in late 1939 meant German attacks on British ships bringing in substantial quantities of imported food. As a result, a rationing system was introduced for items such as bacon, butter, and sugar and later to include meat, eggs, tea, jam, milk, and dried fruits. In this, Bevin played a major role in his new job and was able to negotiate labour mobilization issues within a framework of JPCs and collective bargaining arrangements. This was a vital and tricky balancing act, and was delivered with some success.

The appointment of an outstanding trade union leader – Mr Bevin – as Minister of Labour and National Service was one of the most significant contributions of the trade union movement to the national labour supply policy, and it greatly facilitated the success of that policy.[5]

---

5 N. Barou, *British Trade Unions* (Victor Gollancz, 1947), p.151.

By the end of 1940 the national mood had changed from fearful resentment to grim determination to dig in and win. With Bevin heading up the entire manpower and labour section of the war effort, it appeared that the working class at last had a true representative. This meant that Bevin's version of voluntary bargaining within a set framework between equals was the dominant theme for wartime industrial relations, because 'the key to everything that followed lay in Bevin's claim that the responsibility for all manpower and labour questions must not be broken up but concentrated in the hands of a single minister, himself'.[6] Common cause for more production, more efficient production, and more relevant production was enough, the trade union leaders believed, to deliver a tripartite system that would squeeze out both rogue employers and pesky militants.

In practice much was a botch, with union leaders agreeing to a truce over demarcation and 'other restrictive practices' on the condition they would be allowed to return after the war – a deal that could not be delivered. What was delivered in the here and now was the Emergency Powers Act permitting compulsory deployment of labour. Real labour shortages did not appear until late 1941. In 1940 and 1941 there was a slump in the building trade that disadvantaged many TGWU members, and certainly in these early years of the war, the mass disruption meant great hardship. TGWU members were caught up in the bombing raids and loss of lives and homes. The official line reflected in localities was that it had to be endured, but the leadership did realize that their members 'were paying a big price, working excessive hours, carrying out a great deal of voluntary work, contributing to savings, and helping the country' (*The Record*, April 1940).

> The war had a profound effect on the conditions in which British trade unions had to work. From the beginning the unions pledged themselves to support the fight against Fascism [...]. [W]hile contributing to the war effort the unions could not, and did not, abate their general concern with the conditions of labour.[7]

The TGWU was quite clear that its duty remained to fully contribute to the war effort, to defend workers against exploitation, and to prepare for a major union role in post-war reconstruction. This meant involvement in labour supply and the machinery for dispute resolution; wages and conditions of service; and union participation in war production with a pointer to a future role.

After July 1940, with the outlawing of strikes, pay awards were parsimonious at best. There was some wage improvements among rayon

6 Bullock, *Minister of Labour*, p.12.
7 Barou, *Trade Unions*, p.150.

workers at Courtaulds, in the gas sector, and in seed crushing. Generally, businesses sought to cut wages arguing that everyone had to make sacrifices. This tone infuriated Deakin, and the TGWU were particularly angry with those farmers putting up farm rents while trying to cut farm workers' pay.

In such dark days Deakin and the TGWU leaders were starkly clear as to the nature of the enemy: 'beastly, inhuman, indescribably filthy, and, above all, typically Nazi in its stark brutality, is the attack now being waged against the civilian population of this country' (*The Record*, October 1940). Even then Deakin raised the important issue of a better world after the war, with social justice and social democracy at its heart, with public ownership and control, planning, and the need for an industrial strategy. This was to be based on universal social security and a 'square deal for labour'.

Communists As Enemies and Friends

The TGWU lead the way in attacking all forms of militancy and everything communist. Morrison banned the *Daily Worker* from 21 June 1941 to 27 September 1942, 'and not a dog barked'.[8] The immediate embarrassment caused to government was the communist agitation for better and more accessible air-raid shelters, and improved pay and conditions for members of the armed forces. Sedition indeed.[9]

Deakin's control over the TGWU was linked with the campaign against communists.

> Arthur Deakin was most probably best known to the general public for his campaign against Communists in trade unions. He, more than any other British trade union leader, led the drive against them after the Second World War. Openly and on every conceivable occasion he attacked them for their activities and motives in the British and international spheres of trade unionism.[10]

Rank-and-file activists were in no doubt which way the wind was blowing with regard to anti-communist sentiment in the higher reaches of the union.[11]

Deakin's anti-communism had four pillars: they used the union for their own political ends; their methods conflicted with union practice

8   Taylor, *English History*, p.503.
9   Branson, *Communist Party*, pp.302–312.
10 Allen, *Trade Union Leadership*, p.270.
11 Graham Stevenson, *The Life & Times of Sid Easton* (Friends of Sid Easton, 1991), p.14, on being a TGWU London-based communist cabby.

and policy; their allegiance was to the CPGB and not the union; and he was angered by the behaviour of communists on the union executive.[12] He disliked, naturally, the tendency of the communists to put forward alterative policies as he saw this as spreading disunity. More relevantly he opposed all forms of unofficial action, a running sore in unions from the start. In particular he was convinced that the communists 'infiltrated' union committees through their use of pre-determined policies and tactics. Hardly a sin.

All the usual accusations were compiled in Deakin's note book: using loopholes in the constitution to gain office, being well organized, working hard at grass roots level, and backing strikes. This latter caused Deakin the most anguish. It also supported his thesis of dual loyalties and ulterior motives for the disruption. His inability to get his way on the union's executive through the power of argument also nagged away at him and undermined his reputation as a compromiser and persuader.

All this discomfort was rooted in fear of the power of parallel forces within the union. TGWU members were still engaged in struggle, with over 40 local and factory strikes in 1939 after the official start of war. In 1940 there were numerous strikes, short and small, but widespread and full of intent. The first national shop stewards' conference met in Birmingham in April 1940. This was followed by the People's Convention in January 1941 which called for a broad anti-fascist coalition, greater trade union rights, and better standard of living for all workers. Some inside the TGWU saw this as another CP ploy and sought to expel leading activists from their union posts, such as John Trotter who was part of the Building Trade Group in the Midlands.

The summer months saw the spread of the conflict with war in the Mediterranean and Egypt. On 22 June 1941 Hitler invaded Russia. Operation Barbarossa was the most deadly invasion in history with over 27 million Soviet citizens killed as a result, but eventually it was also one of the great military failures as the German army was defeated and no strategic advantage was secured. Churchill was happy to ally with Stalin and the Red Army and so the war spread again.

The war itself, especially after the Soviet Union's entry, was a popular one. The German invasion of the Soviet Union in June 1941, although not resulting in the opening of a 'second front', nonetheless prompted the government to send a flow of supplies and armaments via the dangerous Murmansk convoys. The TUC assisted this through its 'Help for Russia' fund and maintained close contact with Soviet trade unions through the Anglo-Russian Trade Union Council established in 1941. Until the end of the war,

12 Allen, *Trade Union Leadership*, pp.274–280.

the anti-communism which had been the hallmark of the TUC leadership since 1926 was temporarily abandoned.[13]

The siege of Leningrad was one part of the monstrous killing spree of the Nazis and their supporters. It lasted nearly 900 days from 8 September 1941, with the Nazis aided and abetted by the Finnish Army from the north and Franco's Spanish Blue Division from the south east. About one million Soviet civilians died as a result.

On 6 December 1941 Japan attacked Pearl Harbour and thereby announced the start of a true world war.

With the German invasion of the USSR the Soviets rapidly became our allies, and with that the zealous anti-communism of Deakin and Citrine was put on hold. This meant greater internal unity in dealing with the daily issues confronting TGWU members. This moment in world history enhanced the position of communists in the trade unions, for example, TGWU No. 1 Region elected two communists as representatives on the GEC and they formed the core for the wider left faction. Communists and non-communists alike now supported common union policies in most areas. In March 1942 Bert Papworth was elected to the GEC and then chosen to sit on the all-powerful Finance and General Purposes Committee. In 1944 he was nominated to sit on the TUC's GC alongside Deakin. Deakin kept his anti-communism quiet for now, but his dealings with them on the GEC made him aware of their power and their potential.

The TGWU leadership sent 'greetings to the Soviet Union [...] good wishes and thanks to our Russian comrades in arms' and joined in a variety of friendship and support groups (*The Record*, July 1942). These sentiments allowed the communists inside the TGWU to breathe more freely and redoubled their efforts to secure production increases within a framework of protecting terms and conditions for the members.

The War Economy and Mass Mobilization

Labour shortages again led to pressure to dilute skills, although these were largely resisted. The importance of the super skilled worker for the war effort created the need for the Essential Works Order 302 in March 1941 and meant that such workers could not be sacked, moved, or conscripted. By the end, over 8.5 million workers were so protected. Dock labour was of particular interest to the TGWU and to the war effort. To maintain the flow of goods, especially in Liverpool and Glasgow, Bevin set up the

13 '1939–1945: The Labour Movement and World War Two', *The Union Makes Us Strong: TUC History Online.*

National Dock Labour Corporation. This involved compulsory registration of dockers who had to accept transfers between ports by June 1940.[14] The scheme raised productivity, made most dockers employees of the Ministry, and helped the TGWU keep its position as the dominant union. Deakin was delighted, but the dockers themselves faced harsh conditions and remained deeply antagonistic to the employers. 'Bevin's greatest fear was that labour shortages in the docks and other key industries might reach chaotic proportions [...]. [D]ockers' wages soon rose above the national average, thanks to the high basic rates, the spread of piecework to the Northern ports and long hours of work'. The dilemma was that compulsory measures, while speeding up the process, might create a militant rank-and-file kick back. Bevin decided to 'browbeat and be blessed'.[15]

Work on the dockside remained uncertain and uneven as the war created new patterns of trade. By the end of 1940 dock work was at full tilt in the North East, but progress was hindered by wagon congestion caused by overflowing warehouses. 'There is considerable fluctuation in the volume of employment in this port, as some weeks we have difficulty in filling up the gangs, whilst other weeks there is practically no work at all'.[16]

In general, control over labour came in the form of the Emergency Powers Act in May 1940 which meant industrial conscription by which the minister could require any worker over 16 to be moved where necessary. By the end of 1940 there were still shortages and the call was for women to be conscripted into necessary work, and by the end of 1941 single women and childless widows aged 20–30 were labelled as mobile workers to be sent wherever needed. While strong local union organization and a favourable labour shortage gave unions more strength, the lack of the strike weapon ultimately undermined wage negotiations. Unofficial strike action escalated as a result after 1942.

Over the summer of 1941, with mobilization in full swing, and armaments expanding, the TGWU reported mass membership drives resulting in over one million members. The Royal Ordnance factory at Aycliffe, for example, employed 23,000 women and 4,000 men, with their own stand-alone union branch. Women did indeed flood into the union and were at last both welcomed and catered for more specifically. Recruitment remained patchy and still owed something to the attitude of employers with, for example, US companies such as Ford being less unionized than Standard Motors. This was in part due to employers eyeing joint negotiations and consultations with a withering look – something to

---

14 Jim Phillips, 'British Dock Workers and the Second World War: The Limits of Social Change', *Scottish Labour History*, 1995, no.30, pp.87–103.
15 Wilson, *Dockers*, p.93.
16 NE Area Docks and Waterways Trade Group Committee Minutes, 25 June 1941; Tyne and Wear archives.

Figure 4: Women labourers clearing bomb debris, London, May 1941
Credit: *Daily Worker* archive at Marx Memorial Library

be endured in war but to be forgotten after. JPCs proved to be another
illusion that ended in disillusion.

Bevin said: 'It must be appreciated that in their heart of hearts the
powers that be are anti-union [...]. The Ministers and Departments have
treated Labour with absolute contempt'.[17] But, he argued, without the
unions the army cannot be supplied nor the nation fed. Bargaining power

17 Cited in Lovell and Roberts, *TUC*, p.145.

was transformed by labour shortages, and on 25 May 1940 Bevin set out his proposals to a conference of trade union executives. He stressed that the problem of wage claims and strikes during the war meant keeping existing bargaining machinery, and the use of machinery of binding arbitration when a settlement could not be reached. This was Order 1305. The Treasury wanted direct control over wages, but Bevin wanted to keep it based on normal negotiations. One administrative consequence was that in 1941 the TUC set up its regions to operate in parallel to the government's 12 defence regions, formally becoming TUC regional advisory committees in 1945.

In 1941 Citrine on behalf of TUC made it clear that they would not accept wage stability as it meant falling living standards (*TUC Annual Report* 1941). From 1939–1941 wages lagged behind prices, but by July 1941 wages started to rise and until 1944 earnings rose faster than wages as a result of longer hours and piece rate.[18] Wage increases and war bonuses were negotiated by the TGWU for their members in sectors such as the tin box trade, cocoa and chocolate, gas workers in London, crane operators in Merseyside, and on the waterways. This was very much what the TGWU wanted – settlements industry by industry to avoid any blanket pay controls from central government. A key part of the TGWU's plans to safeguard their members was the Dockers' Charter, and this played well with their insistent demands for more planning and the need for 'a new social order' after the war. Other issues concerned the increase in accidents in factories, especially in engineering and chemicals, and the urgent need to retrain and settle 'disabled persons'.

At the BDC in Llandudno there was strong support from the leadership for the use of compulsory arbitration in the place of the right to strike, and a renewed push to fight for equal pay for women. There was also emphasis on the importance of price stabilization and enhanced social security to control the demand for higher wages. At the TUC Deakin was keen to win over the other unions for the nationalization of transport after the war.

During the first few months of the war, there were over 900 strikes, almost all of them very short but illegal nonetheless. Despite the provisions of Order 1305 there were very few prosecutions until 1941 since Bevin, anxious to avoid the labour unrest of the First World War, sought to promote conciliation rather than conflict. The number of strikes increased each year until 1944. Almost half of them were in support of wage demands, and the remainder against deteriorations in workplace conditions. This went hand in hand with exhortations by Deakin to 'speed up the war effort', and constant reminders of 'what we are fighting for'. In order to restate their democratic credentials and keep the members in

18 Roberts, *National Wages Policy*, p.33.

line, Deakin repeated the ways in which the TGWU was governed: 'the TGWU is a democratic organisation whose government is vested in the general membership' (*The Record*, November 1941).

Order 1305 and Wage Bargaining

Order 1305 banned strikes, and thereby altered the ways in which collective bargaining was conducted across the TGWU units.

> Undoubtedly the war-time expedient which left the greatest imprint on the whole of our voluntary system was the Conditions of Employment and National Arbitration Order, 1940, familiarly known as Order 1305. Part III of the Order helped to enlarge the application of already existing collective agreements, and, in doing so, to strengthen both employer and union organizations.[19]

It meant that arbitration became, for a while anyway, an integral part of the voluntary system. Statutory wage regulation was further cemented under the 1943 Catering Wages Act, 1945 Wages Council Act, and the 1947 Agricultural Wages Act.

In cases of deadlock, after the existing machinery of bargaining had been exhausted, an arbitration tribunal would be able to issue legally binding decisions. The government discouraged all wage fixing bodies to award wage increases if possible, although there was some notion of 'efficiency bargaining' if both sides could show a wage increase was needed to improve productivity.[20] Price controls were seen as the main way to check wages.

> If prices could be stabilised, Bevin argued, it would be possible to keep wage rates steady as well [...]. Henceforward wage policy rested, as the official history puts it, on 'a combination of faith and works – faith in the moderating influence of the trade unions and action to control the cost of living'.[21]

Here was the nub of Deakin's line at the TGWU – a voluntary system of collective bargaining based on moderation of union demands met by reasonable employers and overseen by a benign but aloof state.

The voluntary tradition has been jealously guarded by the liberal left as part of so-called 'collective laissez-faire'. This position came closest

19 Flanders, *Trade Unions*, p.283.
20 Roberts, *National Wages Policy*, p.31.
21 H.M.D. Parker, *Manpower: A Study of War-Time Policy and Administration* (HM Stationery Office, 1957). p.428, cited in Bullock, *Minister of Labour*, p.86.

to realization from 1924–1933, but thereafter state intervention steadily increased in one form or another. This came to a head with Order 1305:

> what we have seen in the British system is (i) a process of sociali-zation in the sense of state intervention in industrial relations, which (ii) took the form of 'administrative regulation' rather than statutory intervention, and (iii) was undertaken with the support of the trade unions'.[22]

With both unions and employers growing larger, the TGWU being a prime example, so it became more expedient for the state to introduce controls. After 1934 the Ministry became more pro-active, and there is 'evidence for this in the willingness to introduce industry-specific legisla-tion to underpin the bargaining process or to create statutory procedures where such arrangements were wanting'.[23] The TGWU-dominated road haulage sector was one example with the Road Haulage Wages Act 1938 consolidating earlier fair wages clauses in legislation. The Minister of Labour claimed it was the government's obligation to 'foster and encourage the establishment of [collective bargaining] machinery over an ever-widening field'.[24]

In terms of industrial relations and trade unionism new patterns emerged. Unions demanded and were granted formal parity with employers in the war effort through joint consultation and negotiation. Wage restraint had to be matched by price controls. A major part of this strategy was to enable union leaders to maintain authority over their local activists. The fear being that other more stringent systems would reduce national union leaders to bystanders as the real business of industrial relations was done at plant level. This was anathema to both Bevin and Citrine as the spectre of communist influence haunted their political wills.

Wartime production systems favoured both trade union growth and shop steward power. Shop stewards became the focus for union activity, bargaining, information, and the link to the national union. Jack Jones recalls:

> drawing on my Liverpool experiences I knew that I had to develop a collective approach to problems. I began to organize classes, in addition to special meetings of shop stewards. The union office became a workshop for the exchange of information and

22 Keith Ewing, 'State and Industrial Relations: "Collective Laissez-Faire" Revisited', *Historical Studies in Industrial Relations*, 1998, vol.5 no.1, pp.1–31, p.16.
23 Ewing, *The State*, pp.26–27.
24 Ernest Brown in Hansard 335 11 May 1938 *c*.162; cited in Ewing, *The State*, p.30.

training of shop stewards, teach-ins, mock negotiating sessions and educational courses were developed.[25]

The trademark policy of the TGWU leadership under Deakin was to maintain the tradition of 'voluntarism' as the standard for all collective bargaining and thereby avoid the pitfalls of a free-for-all in an over-regulated state-sponsored system. It was largely rooted in a notional consensus that responsible big business would prefer negotiation to the uncertainty of pitch battles, and that the interests of the capitalist state as a whole were to be found in industrial peace rather than brutalized conflict. This was later expressed as sharing power in order to keep power, and mirrored the mafia business model of keeping 'one's friends close and one's enemies closer'.

Such dominant consensus was created by ignoring large sections of working-class life and workaday realities. The issue of children's employment during the war, especially in agriculture for example, showed the thin ice upon which common cause existed. Employers and government were in favour as this was a source of cheap and plentiful labour with few rights, while unions opposed seeing it as a way of avoiding employing adults on adult wages.[26]

This was opposed by those on the right unsure of union 'moderation' and those modern statists, such as Beveridge and Keynes, who wanted direct control over wages. Deakin, on behalf of the TGWU, argued in contrast, that direct controls would only stir up discontent on all sides as they sought to ramp up production and hopefully productivity as well.

Trade-union leaders and officers had shown themselves ready to go a long way in pressing their members to put the national interest before sectional advantages – for example in agreeing to set aside hard-won rules and regulations in many industries and in damping down wage claims – but they could only do this if they preserved their authority with the members who paid and employed them.[27]

The TGWU policy initiatives meant unions had to represent their members' interests within realistic limits based on co-operative compromise with employers. Citrine remained suspicious that the government would favour the employers through a form of wage stops.[28] The TGWU

25 Jones, *Jack Jones*, p.93.
26 Stephen Cunningham, 'Reform or Recalcitrance? The Home Office and the Regulation of Child Labour 1939–1951', *Historical Studies in Industrial Relations*, 2002, vol.13, no.1, pp.1–36.
27 Bullock, *Minister of Labour*, p.88.
28 TUC, *The Trade Unions and Wages in War Time* (Co-operative Printing Society, 1941).

wanted wages to remain negotiable at local level in order to allow for the smooth working of factory production under a war economy, which involved skill mix changes, technology improvements, speed-up, shifts in labour markets, and changing demand from government.

Order 1305 allowed, in the classic arbitral fashion, that

> [w]hen the dispute is reported to the Minister he may take steps to secure a settlement by appointing a single arbitrator, or by referring it to the Industrial Court. If all other steps to conciliate the dispute fail, he may refer the dispute to the new National Tribunal which he has set up. This Tribunal consists of a permanent Court of three, and one representative each from the trade unions and the employers.[29]

Crucially, it did not prevent wage demands and did not change the normal method of wage negotiations. This was the entire point of the show – to allow wages to match demand within limits. The main control over wages was not the Order but the government policy on prices as set out in the Price Stabilization and Industrial Policy (Cmd 6294). This allowed the TUC GC to call for wage restraint without wage restraint. Citrine restated his opposition to 'the hoary device of trying to fix wages by regulation'.[30] A technical innovation, the cost-of-living index,[31] helped out by pegging wages to its movements. Deakin was fully aware of the government's fiddling of the figures behind the index in order to disguise price rises and curtail wage increases.[32]

By the summer of 1941 earnings were 43 per cent higher than in October 1938, but wages only 18 per cent higher due to more overtime and piece rate. This lasted to the end of 1944 when demand dropped and pressure on wages fell back. From 1938 to 1945 prices rose by 48 per cent, wage rates by 43 per cent, and earnings by 80 per cent. War work paid better with a narrowing of skills differentials. The overall picture was mixed with dock labourers doing less well, while other TGWU groups did better in transport (trains and lorries), some engineers, and shipbuilders.

Throughout 1942 the TGWU members faced more problems at work, more varied problems, and had fewer means by which to resolve them. The union experienced a large increase in membership with branch life becoming more stressful and harder to deliver members' demands. Deakin and Clay reminded officials that 'better wages and conditions don't just happen' and they needed to 'renew our faith' in 'a sound and healthy

29 *TUC 1940 Annual Report*, p.172.
30 *TUC 1941 Annual Report*, pp.362–363.
31 Peter Field (March 1941), 'The Fraud of the Cost-of-Living Index' (*Labour Monthly*).
32 Allen, *Trade Union Leadership*, p.121.

democracy' with equal opportunities, greater security, an end to elitism, greater civil liberties, and the harnessing of science to improve living standards (*The Record*, February 1942).

The Awkward Case of Provincial Bus Workers:

Bus services were maintained in wartime although much reduced in most areas. The task of keeping buses on the roads was fraught with problems of maintaining an ageing fleet, and on the east coast, crews had to face machine-gun fire. There were about 65,000 bus drivers and related staff, and their terms and conditions were subject to restrictions imposed through Order 1305. There was a more specific arrangement for provincial bus staff from June 1940, known as the 'Standstill Agreement', which allowed for no changes in basic pay and conditions during the war. This started on a favourable basis since the employers had already matched their municipal counterparts by offering bus workers a war bonus of between four and seven shillings a week. War bonuses were awarded to provincial bus workers each year of the war adding 24s 6d on average to their weekly wages.[33]

The senior TGWU officer, Harold Clay, complained that there was a 'lack of understanding' amongst the membership about war wage negotiations. In May 1943, frustration spilled over into unofficial strike action when bus workers walked out. The action began in Yorkshire, spread to the Midlands and then the Thames Valley. The TGWU had called a delegate conference to discuss the rejection of the union's wage claim by the national arbitration tribunal. The resulting strikes spread from Nottingham and Rotherham to Derby, with over 900 workers in Huddersfield and 1,000 in Barnsley involved. The grievance was formally about pay, but there was growing resentment at arbitrary dismissals and harsh punishments for lateness. They quickly fizzled out, but the unions and employers subsequently agreed on an increase of 4s 6d a week. Clay's influence helped persuade his colleagues to accept the settlement, albeit grudgingly and by a narrow majority, when the unions reported back to their members. One factor in this show of militancy was that the provincial workers sometimes shared depots with their better-paid municipal colleagues and thus knew at first hand of the differentials. As Clay remarked, 'we have to remember that men congregate together. There is such a thing as integration of services, sharing common stances, meeting in the same cafe or coffee house, as the case may be, swapping experiences: and it is in those places where some of your difficulties may start'.[34]

33 Temple, "'A Difficult and Peculiar Section'", p.207.
34 Evidence of Harold Clay, Transcript of the Court of Inquiry, 4 March 1946; BET archives, 21178, 33; cited in Temple, "'A Difficult and Peculiar Section'", p.209.

The TGWU at War: Administration and Education

The TGWU under Deakin devolved wartime decision-making to regional secretaries to reduce the reliance on London-based HQ staff. In 1940 and 1941 elections were cancelled due to the churn of members – to the armed forces, doing a stint at civil defence after work, and being moved around the country. Some TGWU officials moved into posts as labour officers especially in the docks. Deakin allowed 22 existing full-time officers to move across. He had to justify this decision since the loss of so many experienced union men was potentially harmful to the membership. Indeed, the TUC asked the government to make union officials a reserved occupation. This was refused. Much of the day-to-day union work was done by branch secretaries, but again such work was disrupted when these were moved around to vital work locations. At the same time the workload for union officials increased as they had to deal with a string of government orders. Union officials had to safeguard their members' rights under wartime controls, as well as dealing with JPCs.

The union came under strain as an institution with a surge in members as well as disrupted branch business. In 1939 TGWU membership stood at 694,474. By 1940 it was 743,349, and then rose and fell: in 1941, it was 948, 079, in 1942 1,133,165, in 1943 1,122,480, in 1944 1,070, 470, and in 1945 1,019, 069.

Most of the recruitment was among general workers, and in metal, engineering and chemicals. Only among dock workers was there decline. This membership expansion was aided by its strong top-down organizational model. More important was full employment under which workers can pay their subs and be active without fear of victimization. Women in particular sought the safety of being in a union. Most growth was in sectors already well served by strong shop stewards, and their recruitment overtures were hard to resist. The second main reason for union growth was the particular nature of the Essential Work Orders and Conditions of Employment and National Arbitration Order. These meant that the special circumstances of essential work protected union activists, and unions were often sounded out by the Ministry before granting a firm the benefits of the schedule. Thus 'bad' employers might fall foul of union opinion and lose out on contracts. Such indirect 'contract compliance' gave rise to later moves for such state assurances.

The TGWU, with its vast army of full-time officials, was able to gain the most from such arrangements. Union recognition was not a formal requirement for firms to win contracts, but it became a useful prop for those wishing to gain a commercial advantage. Order 1305 allowed for industrial disputes to be referred to arbitration. In practice this was used to pressurize anti-union firms, the majority, into recognition to stave off expensive arbitration cases. Once in the factories, union officials could recruit and create a virtuous circle of solving disputes, growing the union, encouraging lay activists, and thereby strengthening union presence.

One effect of wartime production was that women and young workers were more likely to work shifts and at night. Again employers needed permits for such conditions and TGWU officials could enter the factories to negotiate these and thus recruit women and youths into the union.

JPCs also provided a fertile field in which to recruit. Most of their members were active trade unionists. Despite such favourable conditions for union growth from 1943–1945 TGWU membership fell back. On 6 December 1943 Deakin reported the reasons to the GEC: 'closure of certain factories, with a transference of members to other employment and a consequent loss of contracts [...] growing feeling that we are nearing the end of the war' as well as the trend to wage stabilization.[35] An additional factor was that the earlier surge in membership could not be handled by the union's organizational systems, and therefore some new members did not reap any benefits from the union.

Deakin was concerned with the union finances since these were the key to membership numbers, sound administration, and the basis upon which the union was fully represented on numerous national and regional bodies. In the TGWU it is the regional secretaries who are the gatekeepers. They collect contributions and from these pay all benefits (except strike and victimization) and all regional running costs. The main costs were salaries of officials, and these were kept under strict central control. The regional secretaries reported fortnightly and in greater detail quarterly to the centre. Funds could be increased either through recruitment of members at regional level, or by putting up subs, a decision taken at national level. Deakin's view of having a war chest was clear: 'money does talk, in dealing with employers; they are always more ready to fight when the workers have nothing to fight with' (recalled BDC to increase subs by 1d a week, October 1942) (*The Record*, November 1942).

Deakin was also aware that there was a large upsurge in his members' resentment at pay restraints, and that he wanted a large strike fund for the anticipated strike wave after the war. Overall the TGWU finances were stable with steady revenues from contributions and constant outgoings as there had been no strike since the busmen in 1937. In 1942 the general fund was just over £2 million, rising to nearly £3.5m by 1945. Administrative costs represented about three-fifths of all expenditure during the war years.

The GEC was constantly worried about controlling expenditure at regional level. Bevin did it through a formula linking regional sub

---

35 Acting General Secretary report to GEC, December 1943, cited in Allen, *Trade Union Leadership*, p.229.

revenues to expenses, but this was rather rough and ready. Deakin, in contrast, was less rigid but far more watchful. His ability to maintain an even settlement depended on his good relations with regional secretaries themselves, and on the central union efficiencies being equal to those in the regions – leading by example. A key factor in administrative stability was the rate of membership turnover and linked problem of arrears. Such churn was a major drain on resources. The combination of natural wastage (retirees) and non-renewal when moving jobs was a running sore. Administrative failings were partly to blame alongside the level of trade union consciousness among general labourers. This played into both the need for more education and better communication of union benefits, but also into a more political and ideological approach to agitation and representation.

Deakin was a hands-on leader, but this had no impact on the running costs of central office, at about 10 per cent of income. Union salaries remained the largest cost item hovering around 25 per cent of revenues. During the war years Deakin effectively controlled all such salaries from the centre. Not until 1947 were formal national negotiations over staff and officials salaries made. His rather obtuse stance meant that TGWU officials' salaries lagged behind both other unions and their own members.

'Each Regional Committee wanted sufficient full-time officials and staff to tackle its own problems',[36] and Deakin sought to balance these against the overall union need. The pressure was building to further develop the trade group system, but at the 1943 BDC Deakin opposed any increase in staff already in post. Crucial to Deakin's hold over the union was his relationship with the powerful regional secretaries. As in most unions, ultimate authority lies with Conference, but in between these events the GEC was in power (Rule 6.13, TGWU constitution).

Deakin was a member of the GEC *ex officio* but was the most powerful voice. His power over the GEC stemmed from his day-to-day presence in the office running union matters with a detailed knowledge of what was required. This allowed him to generally move the GEC and the Finance and General Purposes Committee in the direction he wanted. His second advantage over the GEC was that he was a permanent fixture while there was greater turnover of GEC members. The real Deakin factor was his formidable skills as a report presenter and defender, a determination to push ahead, and his powerful aura of control and command. In addition the job of general secretary, along with that of finance secretary, are the only two jobs with constitutional recognition. Other regional and HQ officials had only vague duties assigned by rule. Deakin, unlike Bevin, found it hard to delegate and was more interested in details, but like Bevin

---

36 Allen, *Trade Union Leadership*, p.247.

he immensely enjoyed the power he wielded. His authoritarian streak was witnessed at TGWU and TUC conferences where he sought to control debate, influence his own delegates, and dominate proceedings.

As a result Deakin and the TGWU leadership around him were heavily criticized as being bureaucratic in a bad way. The attacks were based on the union being over-centralized, slow to change, that communications were inadequate and unclear, and that senior figures had become divorced from the concerns of the rank-and-file membership. Large size comes with institutional complexity in which officials are appointed rather than elected and dissent is seen as disloyal. An over-rigid and legalistic use of the rules becomes the hallmark of control and political attacks the feature of coercion. Like some real world Gormenghast, the keeper of the rule book is the power in the land.

Education

A crucial aspect of the development of the TGWU at the time was the quality of branch officials.[37] Quality here refers to the ability to organize and manage branch matters, represent members, and play their part in union reputation building. A central concern has been the education of such officials in order to make them and keep them fit for their roles. Deakin started to invest in internal educational facilities with the appointment of a full-time secretary in 1938, and the union funded both the WEA the NCLC. In 1939 the union started its own 'postal' study course, 'The Union, its Work and Problems'.

This was Bevin's initiative but Deakin took it over and developed it into a more thorough-going programme. Overall,

> despite the war situation, the Home Study course flourished, and the provision of union-only day schools rose to a peak in 1945. The unionisation of women was also strengthened in the war years, and a new generation of local leaders, typified by Jack Jones in Coventry, began to use trade union education in new ways linked to workplace organisation and the increasingly important role being played by shop stewards.[38]

Just before the official declaration of war, applications for the correspondence course had reached nearly 2,000. The GEC decided, nonetheless, to suspend its operation, although Bevin reversed this decision in November.

37 Joseph Goldstein, *The Government of a British Trade Union: A Study of Apathy and the Democratic Process in the Transport and General Workers Union* (George Allen & Unwin, 1952).
38 Fisher, *Bread on the Waters*, p.65.

Over 1,600 enrolled, mainly from London, the North West, and from Passenger and General Workers' groups.

Most students, however, had been forced to quit the course due to national service, overtime increases, and more union work. The GEC kept it going with nearly 200 union members completing by the end of the year. The Education Committee was committed to high standards and this became more apparent during the war when there was some temptation to relax. In 1941 another 250 students went through the course, and in 1942, with an invasion no longer likely, there were over 3,300 applications. At the time the course was a success, but it was static and limited and amounted to little more than reading and writing about the union.

John Price promoted his ideas through *The Record* in the summer of 1941. Here he argued for the importance of union education in the deeper and wider fight for a better future for the working class. He developed, through the Education Committee, an extra part of the syllabus focusing on trade union development since 1914, and then detailing the debates about the role of unions in wartime. The course itself was a failure with very few recruits and it closed in 1944. The thinking behind 'The Union and the War' was to promote non-communist progressive ideas by laying down markers for future battles within the TGWU over political dissent and industrial struggles.

The WEA and the NCLC had run weekend schools where learning took place through interactive face-to-face discussion. The TGWU could not mimic such provision, but there were parallel developments. Fisher outlines three types of schools: there were schools for the purpose of organizing and supporting shop stewards, and Jack Jones in Coventry and Tom Wylie in Birmingham were at the forefront of such initiatives. Secondly, was the genuine study group based at branch level to help each other with the correspondence courses; and thirdly, there were national day schools with senior figures lecturing while touring the country.[39] The first instance of this national showcase was in January 1940 in London with Deakin accompanied by Price and Clay. This highly successful start-up was well received, and others soon followed. In March 1940 another school was held in Hanley (Stoke-on-Trent) with over 70 local TGWU members.

Throughout 1941 and 1942 such events took place 'as and when' across the country. They were good opportunities for the leadership, especially Deakin, to push both his ideas about trade unionism and himself as a sympathetic leader. By 1944 their success was secure. Such educational systems had become embedded in the national strategic plan for the future of the TGWU after the war. Meanwhile the lesser study groups continued to perform a more prosaic function, and focused on

39 Fisher, *Bread on the Waters*, p.72.

the union itself with, for example, material on the union's structure later reproduced in *The Record* in November 1941 and morphing into a booklet, *Introducing the TGWU*. This latter had a print run of 40,000 copies with spin offs entitled, *What is the TGWU?* and, *Yes, but why should I join?*

Jack Jones was singled out for his outstanding contribution to the union in Coventry and for his pioneering work linking union education with organization and struggle. He understood that such educational activities performed several tasks: they brought members together and helped maintain production in the car industry after the blitz; they allowed activists to become local leaders, and they created a more informed set of discussions among the wider membership about key industrial relations' issues. He explained that collecting subs in 'pub nights' meant an opportunity to persuade the shop stewards of the benefits of training.

Tom Wylie in Birmingham and Charles Brandon in London came at the problem from a slightly different angle. They was already part of the wider adult education movement with involvement in the WEA and local adult colleges. In Bristol they developed a particular model way of working with six linked lectures and a library. Women activists, Florence Hancock and Ellen McCullough, played a leading part in these innovations. Indeed, Florence Hancock had already been moved to central office in 1939 having been women's officer for Area 3. She became National Women's Officer for service with the metal, chemical and engineering group and the General Workers Group in November 1942. She was the main tutor for women-only TGWU day schools. By the end of 1944 women convenors could be found at the heart of struggle at GEC in Coventry, Rolls Royce at Hillingdon, and at G & J Weir in Glasgow.

In June 1943 the union held a special national delegate conference for women only. A priority was all-women's schools for union education, with such an event for women in the aircraft industry in Rochester on 15 January 1944 led by Ellen McCullough.

> The union had tapped into the great release of energy which the war had produced, and by 1945 the number of TGWU students on the correspondence course, the day schools and WETUC [Workers' Educational Trade Union Committee] and NCLC courses was the highest ever [...] for the union education programme, the real task was to consolidate the gains and to keep the new link between education, union organisation and development.[40]

---

40 Fisher, *Bread on the Waters*, p.88.

The View from the Members on the Ground

I must keep fightin' until I'm dyin'
(Paul Robeson's own version of the lyrics from Ol' Man River)

Many workers, including TGWU members, were caught up in the dangers and inconveniences of wartime Britain. These included road accidents due to problems with headlight use, explosions in factories and dockyards, air-raid duties, helping with the increasing number of refugees, and navigating the rules and regulations of everyday life. Yet, despite the sanguine noises from head office, the reality in the docks in Bristol, Southampton, London, Belfast, and Glasgow was much harsher. Reports from 1940 show that thousands of dockers were being overworked and underpaid. Some employers were ignoring the government's agreement that while away from home dockers should receive 10s a day standing-by money.

In Bristol, for example, the TGWU officials were of little use: 'conditions in this port are scandalous and the worst in the country[...] Usually one or two of the trade union officials attend the Disciplinary Board – which is presided over by a local ship owner – but very seldom speak or do anything in defence of their members' (*Daily Worker*, 19 April 1940). In April further troubles on the docks followed in Belfast over work sharing and the layoff of skilled men, and in Southampton over employers' efforts to extend the working day. By the summer the situation was no better as London dockers demanded work in line with government regulations in order to protect union terms and conditions from employers using non-union men to undermine agreements. Over 400 TGWU dockers marched on their own union offices to demand the transfer scheme was enforced.

On 21 October 1940 it was reported that 'Glasgow dockers have won a very big victory on the question of registration. After the union had given in on the question, the men continued to resist' (*Daily Worker*, 21 October 1940). These reports of disgruntled dockers are reflected in the statistics. There were 30 strikes in each of the war years as a reflection of formal opposition, and informal discontent was reflected with absenteeism reaching 30 per cent at times in the Liverpool docks. The employer-requested 'Continuity Rule' and the end of casualization did not resolve the distinct differences between unions and employers over control of workload and working time.[41]

41 The Continuity Rule was part of a complex web of formal and informal practices associated with the hiring of dock labour on a casual basis. The notion, which had contradictory outcomes, was that once engaged in loading/unloading a vessel, the docker is both entitled and required to complete the work for which he was engaged.

On the buses and trams it was not much better with reports of workers being 'hard hit' and members' demands for united action across the passenger transport group. By late August the Bethnal Green branch 1/474 of the TGWU demanded that buses did not run after the air-raid warning had been sounded. By Christmas, busmen in the North East were pushing for wages to catch up with prices. The United Company were making large profits but these were not being shared with the workers. Other shop-floor struggles continued apace despite the TGWU national leadership's lack of involvement. In October there was a strike of over 600 men and women in a Scottish aero-engine plant over the TGWU's right to organize women.

Towards the year end, the TUC leaders further antagonized their activists by bestowing the Gold Medal for services to the union movement on King George VI. A typical rally of working-class activists in Glasgow shouted down Ernest Bevin as he announced restrictions on workers' rights. He was visiting several workplaces in Scotland and attacked unofficial working-class resistance His opponents accused him of helping the government curtail worker rights.

Jack Jones recalls that on 14 November 1940 he attended a meeting with the management of Humber-Hillman in Coventry. The vital question was factory working after the sirens had sounded. This issue of working through bombing raids and the provision of air-raid precautions had been a concern throughout the autumn. The bombing of Coventry killed thousands and disrupted work and the work of the union. Over 20 factories had been damaged and that meant no work for large numbers of TGWU members. Jones lamented that 'trade union branch life was totally disorganized'. The main channel of communication was through shop stewards, although most managers made it difficult for them to function in the workplace. Jones visited Singer Motors which had suffered direct bombing. The importance of a strong TGWU presence in the locality was shown when Standard Motors changed over to aircraft production and they poached men from Armstrong Whitworth Aircraft. Jones was part of the negotiations on transfers and as he argues by being there the union achieved both the unionization of a largely non-union workforce, and through a collective system of piecework achieved both higher output and higher earnings.[42]

Air raids and losses at sea were compounded by problems on the railways in the winter 1940–1941. Nonetheless,

The workers did not feel this time that they were being exploited for a bosses' war. They, too, were ready for sacrifice, though they expected a policy of 'fair shares' and, on the whole, got it. War

42 Jones, *Jack Jones*, pp.99–104.

socialism was socialism by consent, that is to say, socialism with the difficulties left out.[43]

The TGWU put all its resources into maintaining production and the flow of goods. It continued to 'serve' its members throughout the regions and sectors by fully participating in JPCs and collective bargaining arrangements. The most important shift in TGWU policy, once the threat of invasion had been lifted, was the support for the USSR and its abatement of its anti-communist practices.

Bevin and the TGWU now went their own ways, separate but still joined. He had achieved, as he saw it, the great advance of having the working class, through its trade unions, securing 'its proper place in the nation'.[44] His autocratic rule over the union was matched by his organizing skills and the monumental union he had built to last. And so it did.

43 Taylor, *English History*, pp.507–508.
44 Murray, *T&G Story*, p.81.

5

1942–1945: The World War

Introduction

This chapter deals with the world war when both the USA and USSR became fully involved. The war economy meant more favourable conditions for wage bargaining, and when this was not forthcoming from official systems there were more and more unofficial strikes. The role of working women dramatically changed. The push for independence in the colonies and beyond also fed into the desire for a new world order after the war. This became a concrete reality with plans for post-war reconstruction predicated on full employment and 'cradle to grave' social security and health system. It ends with a Labour landslide in the general election and the vindication of everything for which the TGWU had fought.

The Bloodiest of Wars

In January 1942 the 'United Nations' declaration was issued (it was formally established in October 1945) with the USA and the UK as allies in the war along with the Soviets. All agreed to work together to end the war together. In February 1942 Singapore fell, and Burma and Malaya were soon lost to the Axis powers. This Japanese expansion gave renewed vigour to communist-led national liberation movements in the region with Ho Chi Minh leading the Viet Minh, and Mao Zedong, after emerging as the head of the Long March, captaining the Red Army's successful attack on the Japanese (Hundred Regiments Campaign) in August 1940. These developments partly explain the USA's greater interest in the Far East than that of the British generals.

India was another centre of interest – the British feared, without good reason, a Japanese advance and sought to win over Indian popular support. The Americans disliked British Imperial attitudes on the subcontinent, and the British labour movement supported Indian independence as part of its wider commitment to internationalism, although officially nervous about communist domination of Indian trade unions.

In February 1942 the Allies started to bomb German factories but it was not as successful as later depicted, and therefore an invasion of mainland Europe was required. This was based on a strategic agreement with the Americans in April 1942, and early preparations were underway when the humiliating defeat at Tobruk stalled other plans. Montgomery took over the eighth army in North Africa in the autumn, and the Battle of Alamein turned the tide in one theatre of war while the deadly Battle of Stalingrad (August 1942–February 1943), with its two million casualties, was the beginning of the end for the German army. Churchill's main focus was defeating Hitler, and to that end he visited Stalin four times but still refused to open the second front.

Meanwhile, a crisis in domestic coal production brought about early skirmishes over nationalization and any future industrial strategy. The war remained very much a people's war with mass support. National media played a vital role in political life with the *Daily Mirror* the paper of choice for the mass of workers. BBC radio was a constant source of information and entertainment with popular shows such as *ITMA* (It's That Man Again) and the songs of Gracie Fields. The cinema played its part with a raft of 'propaganda' films of exceptional quality including *The Great Dictator, The Grapes of Wrath,* and *Casablanca.*

While workers and their union representatives at local level were holding the fort against bad management and compliant leaders, the full horrors of Nazism were emerging into the public domain. By now news of atrocities against civilians, including Jews, Gypsies, all non-whites, the disabled, and dissenters both religious and secular, was becoming widely broadcast. The Jewish Socialist Bund based in the Warsaw Ghetto fed information to the Soviets, and by December 1942 the Allies had published a stark proclamation about the mass murders and the fate that awaited the perpetrators. The British labour movement was as shocked as everyone else by the atrocities.

The ferocious and deadly Battle of Stalingrad was over by February 1943. The German 6th Army was defeated, and the Soviets could at last turn to victory and life after the war. It was now that the reality of the objective of 'unconditional surrender' became hard currency, thereby reassuring the Soviets that no deal would be done with the Nazis. Popular sentiment throughout Europe was behind such a view of those responsible for unleashing such horrors on the world. By the summer of 1943 world leadership moved from Great Britain to the United States. British strength was waning, and the decisive turn in the war at sea against the U-boats was delivered by American destroyers protecting convoys, the use of British bombers, and Portugal finally allowing the Allies to use the Azores air base.

The summer saw the landing in Sicily, and the overthrow and later execution of Mussolini. The mass bombing of German industrial centres continued apace with Hamburg, the Ruhr, and Berlin targeted. This policy was literally hit and miss with as many town centres destroyed as factories. Churchill pushed for victory in 1944, but Roosevelt was more interested in defeating the Japanese and accommodating the Soviet views of victory in Europe. At the Teheran meeting of the leaders at the end of November 1943 it was the Americans and Soviets who controlled both the agenda and the strategy – Churchill focused on the Mediterranean war theatre rather than opening up a second front. While death and disaster were played out in the battle fields and concentration camps, British workers were spurred on to fight for an end to the war and for a better future. The unions played a vital role in both keeping production flowing and fighting for a more equal and just society.

At the start of 1944 victory was in sight, but remained elusive. This was partly due to divisions between the British and Americans on war priorities. Italy had fallen and Germany was on the back foot, but the Americans were as concerned with the Far East as with Europe. The bombing campaign under Harris was scaled back as its effectiveness was doubted. In Anzio, in January, the battle plan to liberate Rome stalled, but eventually, on 4 June, the Allies did enter Rome. This success was eclipsed by the D-Day landings (operation Overlord) in France two days later.

Just as relief was the sense most evident among the British, the 'doodlebug' bombs (V1 and V2) started to rain down from 13 June 1944 to 27 March 1945. Over 2,300 hit London with nearly 5,500 deaths and 16,000 injuries. The people and the country were exhausted and running out of resources. It was the Americans that took over both sourcing the war effort and commanding the actual war. With the second front becoming a reality in May, Churchill was able to visit Stalin in Moscow to discuss the final assault on the Germans, and tentatively agree the division of Europe after the war.

Against the world stage the TGWU was starting to make demands associated with the war end. These included concerns over the reinstatement of ex-servicemen into their old jobs, and in particular the need for a planned housing policy. This latter was reported in January 1944 with the support of the TGWU's Building Trade Group Committee of Area 1, and endorsed by Deakin, who emphasized the need for the compulsory purchase of land and the involvement of local authorities in housebuilding.

The TGWU leadership repeated their commitments to end mass unemployment, secure 'freedom from want', plan the economy through nationalization, ensure health and education provision for all, win greater equality for women, and establish 'cradle to grave' security. This was the 'new social order' for which Deakin, Price, Clay, and others had fought, and were prepared to defend against the counteroffensive by the Conservatives.

Wartime Collective Bargaining and Strikes

At home the pressures were building on the government's capacity to deliver the necessary levels of war production. All wartime strikes were illegal under Order 1305, and the anger, particularly about wages, spilled over into increasing numbers of stoppages. 'Between mid-1943 and the landing in France on 6 June 1944 there were as many strikes as in the worst period of the first war'.[1] Moreover, 'it is often the Trade Union officials who have had to bear the brunt of the workers' discontent and irritation'.[2] While wages were the up-front issue, there was discontent over delays caused by the national machinery, indifferent officials, and non-pay issues. The union hierarchy tried to smear the strikers as disruptive 'reds', and the counter-charge from the strikers was that the TGWU had promised much and delivered little.

> In 1943 there were two major stoppages, one was a strike of 12,000 bus drivers and conductors and the other of dockers in Liverpool and Birkenhead. Both were a considerable embarrassment to Bevin since they involved mainly TGWU members. 1944 marked the peak of wartime strike action with over two thousand stoppages involving the loss of 3,714,000 days' production. This led to the imposition of Defence Regulation 1AA, supported by the TUC, which now made incitement to strike unlawful.[3]

Strikes in these years rose steadily year-on-year with metal and allied trades a major contributor. In 1940 there were 922 strikes (229 in metal, engineering and shipbuilding); 1941, 1,251 strikes (472 in metal etc); 1942, 1,303 strikes (476 in metal etc); 1943, 1,785 strikes (612 in metal etc); and in 1944, 2,194 strikes (610 in metal etc). And,

> during the Second World War, when strikes were again made illegal, the number of strikes rose sharply, yet because these strikes were of a different character from the 1920s, being short, small, and unofficial, the number of striker days remained at the low level of the 1930s.[4]

Implementation of Order 1305 was haphazard. There were over 1,200 unofficial stoppages by 1941 but only six actions against the strikers in the

---

1 Taylor, *English History*, p.566.
2 Knowles, *Strikes.*, p.37.
3 Roberts, *National Wages Policy*, p.37.
4 Ken Coates and Tony Topham, *Trade Unions in Britain* (Fontana, 1988), pp.232–233.

form of fines and being bound over. The government's own law officers, in consultation with Bevin, were unhappy that there was no real enforcement and that employers were using threats of the provisions to browbeat discontent workers. The confusion in the Order and the one-sided preference for the employers over the workers came to a head. 'A strike in the Betteshanger colliery in Kent in 1942 prompted the first mass prosecutions under Order 1305. Three officials of the Betteshanger branch were imprisoned and over a thousand strikers were fined'.[5]

In August 1939 a regulation was passed allowing troops to be used in emergencies in civilian industrial sectors such as agriculture. 'Regulation Six was made under section 1 of the Act on 28 September 1939 and amended in 1942 to the following form, which remained in force until 1959'.[6] The shift in emphasis was from agriculture only to 'other such work', which allowed the military to intervene directly and legally in any sector of the economy, and that would include breaking strikes.

Deakin was furious at unofficial strikers and urged TGWU members, despite clear and present hardships, to always follow the official collective bargaining routes. The strike statistics for the war years show some shifts. In shipbuilding, a strike-prone sector, for example, the war saw strikes petering out. In contrast, in engineering there were more strikes, linked with dilution and speed-up. The advent of US-style management created a complex web of wage systems causing the majority of strikes. Dockers' tendency to strike was rooted in the casual nature of employment and unusually brutal employers. The war brought an end to casualization through the brokered deal dockers would transfer to other ports in exchange for registration and a guaranteed week. This in turn meant union branches were disrupted and union control over their members reduced to a shambles in some areas.

Road transport, another important section of the TGWU, was under-regulated during the war with nearly 20 per cent of workers being underpaid from 1940–1943. The chaotic state of the industry characterized by small firms meant that pressure was mounting and there was an outpouring of discontent during the first national strike in 1947.

One feature of strikes during this period was the active role of women workers. Knowles suggests: 'it is clear that women [...] have played an important part in strike movements'.[7] Their willingness to 'down tools' and their greater sense of exploitation made them as militant as their equivalent male co-workers. This militancy was to be found in other countries as well such as France, China, Russia, and the USA.

5 '1930–1945: The Labour Movement and World War Two', *The Union Makes Us Strong: TUC History Online.*

6 Steve Peak, *Troops In Strikes* (Cobden Trust, 1984), p.51.

7 Knowles, *Strikes*, p.182.

It was partly due to Bevin's own softly-softly approach that illegal strikes were settled out of court. They were seen as a 'safety valve' allowing some steam to escape while keeping a cap on more dangerous eruptions of discontent. Most of the action was concentrated in coal and engineering, but members of the TGWU in transport, manufacturing, the docks, metals, and chemicals were also involved. In these sectors, generally, wages rose in line with the extra hours worked. Working families were better off after 1942 when the cost of living stabilized, and areas such as the Midlands benefited the most. Some of the gains were due to union strength, but others relied on government action in the docks and on the farms. Women's wages also surged ahead of peacetime rates, and part of this trend was the increase in the rates for semi-skilled and unskilled workers as they closed the gap on increasingly disgruntled skilled colleagues. Nonetheless, 'for all the appearance of unity and direction under Citrine, Bevin, and later Deakin, the war had done little to alter the fragmented and decentralized character of the British industrial relations system'.[8]

An important aspect of long working hours and production pressures was worsening health and safety and compromised welfare at work. The war brought forth canteens, nurseries, and expanded numbers of welfare and medical workplace officers. This new-found interest allowed the TGWU leaders to portray such progress as an ideal to be rolled out as best practice. While such betterment was indeed patchy, the concerns with workplace welfare fed into the wider demands for nationalization of health, education, care, and those industries that underpinned these new beginnings such as energy and transport.

In September 1943 mobilization had peaked, with over 22 million citizens in the armed forces, civil defence, and industry. This meant there was no room for manoeuvre and the working assumption in government was that they could just manage if the war ended in late 1944. As a result of tightening labour markets and joint regulation from March 1942 to July 1945, wages rose for dock labourers from 115 to 123 (100 = 1939); engineers' labourers from 126 to 154; lorry drivers from 119 to 135; and on average from 127 to 152, while prices rose from 129 to 134. It was clear that wages did not match the usual levels associated with such favourable conditions. With union leaders tied into joint regulation and strikes outlawed, it meant scope for local activists to represent the frustrations of some workers and to test the resolve of the TGWU leaders.

Shop stewards inside the TGWU played a leading role in focusing workers on the war effort, in demanding pay improvements, fighting for worker rights, and spreading the struggle beyond the workplace to the national theatre of government policy. Communists were at the centre of much of this, and that is why when the war was coming to a close, the

---

8 Field, *Blood, Sweat and Toil*, p.125.

union leaders, especially in the TUC and TGWU, turned all their guns on their own left-wing activists.

Jack Jones recalls a run in with Arthur Deakin about the registration of skilled workers over the running sore of dilution. The decision from on high was made without consultation. It was a carve-up of union membership lists for the convenience of national leaders, and Deakin refused to shift his position despite protests from local activists. These years saw a transformation in the attitudes of many factory workers towards trade unionism, with elected stewards calling committee meetings in working hours (the blackout made it difficult otherwise), and reporting back to the members as to what was happening both inside the union and with management. As Jack Jones and others have recalled, this new-found union strength improved productivity as mismanagement and inefficiencies were called to account by worker representatives eager to promote the war effort without profiteering

The view from the ground was shifting as defeat was now unlikely and winning the war was a matter of time and resources. Minds turned to both the here and now of working-class struggle, and the possibilities of a just post-war settlement. The immediate pressing issue was war production, and as resources were stretched so productivity increases were a central aim of the war effort. With the Soviets fighting off the Nazi invasion at immense loss of life, the British Left called for a second front, and that required even more production. TGWU activists were exhausted and exasperated by continued poor management and backward-looking employment practices. TGWU members and activists fought for a greater say on the shop floor in the running of enterprises. Such calls were resisted both by local employers fearful of any challenge to their managerial prerogative, and from TGWU leaders who believed in top-down regulation and national committees.

Reluctant employers included Dunlop Rim and Wheel Company which remained staunchly anti-union. After pressure from the local TGWU, the factory was unionized. Jack Jones recalls:

> Co-operation between the shop stewards and the new production committees kept management on its toes on production and supply matters [...] At the Armstrong Whitworth Aircraft Baginton works, for instance, all parties combined to meet high officials of the Ministry of Aircraft Production and the Ministry of Labour in order to discuss material shortages and labour displacement.[9]

He goes on to recount how trade unionism grew rapidly in the Coventry area based on unity and successful fights with those employers still

9 Jones, *Jack Jones*, p.110.

unwilling to come to terms with worker involvement. Most of the disputes at the time were over either piecework or victimization and related disciplinary matters. One firm, Cornercrofts, made aero parts and the local Conservative MP was a director. They sacked 172 workers over the 1941 Christmas holidays for deficient timekeeping but after a short strike, all were reinstated.

The role of women was more openly debated and more thoroughly discussed than at any other time by women active in their unions, communities, and political parties. Jack Jones again gives both a political and personal flavour to events:

> Evelyn, my wife, who was working in the factory at the time as a part-time worker, was asked to put the women's case to the convenor [...]. [T]his she did and was told to 'piss off'. The story behind the rebuff was that the TGWU men were on higher rates than the women and wanted no part in their demands for equal treatment.[10]

He further explains that the TUC and Ministry of Labour gave permits to union officials to visit any firm engaged in government work, and therefore he had access to Imperial Foundry at Leamington. This was a subsidiary of the anti-union USA giant, Ford. The company's founder, Henry Ford was a fascist sympathizer and vicious anti-Semite, and even in the UK encouraged his company police to rough handle trade unionists. 'The Kingdom of Henry Ford is a fascist state [...] All the characteristics of Fascism – Jew-baiting, corruption, gangsterism – exist today wherever King Henry Ford reigns over American workers'.[11] Hitler was an avowed admirer, and Ford had many friends and allies among British factory owners.

The union story in 1942 and 1943 was one of full employment and pressure building on officials to negotiate improvements in pay and conditions to match the strengthening position. This was not forthcoming. Where government intervention was more direct, for example in clay and the waterways, conditions were just about maintained. In sections, such as on the Northern and Gateshead trams, women were put on local JIC rates, but overall pay improvements were sluggish.

Deakin strongly advocated the twin track approach of greater state regulation and ownership and a place at the table for the organized working class represented by the unions. By 1944 that seemed plausible.

---

10   Jones, *Jack Jones*, pp.113–114.
11   Elizabeth Esch, From the Melting Pot to the Boiling Pot: Fascism and the Factory-State at the River Rouge Plant in the 1920s', in Elizabeth Esch (ed.), *The Color Line and the Assembly Line* (California University Press, 2018), pp.51–82.

The Labour Party certainly matched the mood of the country with its support for full employment and comprehensive free welfare, and appeared to support a fair share for all under the 'social justice' banner. The union leaders wanted to keep their voluntary tradition, later dubbed 'free collective bargaining', but within a more favourable national framework. If there was full employment, that in itself, they believed, would strengthen the bargaining position of their members. If there was also a larger social wage through free health and education and subsidized energy and transport, then the pressure for actual wage increases could be held in check. This entire edifice of practical thought was predicated on keeping the ever-more popular communists at bay – by joining the capitalist club as partners they seemed to have cracked the long-standing conundrum of the labour movement: reform without revolution, and progress without Bolshevism.

Equal Rights and the Wartime TGWU: Women and the Colonies

Equality, justice, fairness, and rights to a better life were spoken of within the TGWU as the necessary outcomes of the war. This applied to the working class as a whole, but within that category there was some focus on women at home and workers in the colonies.

This chapter cannot match the real world of those who lived through the war years, and it cannot tell the tale of women's work in any detail. With more women at work came a parallel trend to greater trade unionism. In 1935 only 2 per cent of the women in engineering were in unions, but by 1940 this had increased to 6 per cent. In 1944 there were over nine million women in industrial occupations. More than half the workers in chemical and explosive manufacturing and more than a third in engineering were women. Only slightly in excess of a tenth of women employees were unionized in industries such as aircraft production, marine and general engineering. Membership was heavily concentrated in larger, well-organised establishments. The TGWU committee at Derby Railway Workshops, for example, reported in 1941:

> Women were being engaged at all of occupations at the women's rate of pay and it was felt that women doing simple labouring jobs and crane driving etc., should be on the rate for the job as paid to men and not be either on the women's rate or subject to the craftsmen's dilution agreement.

According to Mary Davis:

> The war accorded women workers a high profile. Conscription for women was introduced in 1941. They had either to work in the munitions (or other designated) industry or were recruited

into the Land Army. This did not mean that the state, in spite of some temporary concessions, had any intention of meaningfully addressing women's 'double burden'. An uneasy contradiction existed in the official mind between the obvious necessity to maintain wartime production on the one hand, and on the other the desire not to destabilise women's role in the family. It manifested itself in an unwillingness to ensure any lasting or general changes to the social order in favour of meeting the needs of working wives and mothers.[12]

The long-term basis for women's unionization in engineering in the West Midlands now came into play, with Coventry munitions workers setting the pace. The union's 300,000 women members started to present 'awkward' demands for decent facilities in factories as well as raising the issue of equal pay. The first conference of women union stewards took place in London on 5 October 1941 and another in Birmingham in April 1942. By 1943 the TGWU had established 44 branches in Derbyshire. This growth was mainly based on the recruitment of women for war work. The union strengthened its base in engineering so, for example, the railway workshop branch had 885 members and had managed to secure no less than six representatives on the overall Railway Shops' Committee. In particular the union made progress in hitherto anti-union employers, such as at Ley's Malleable Castings, and had some 3,500 members at the British Celanese establishments in Derby, Long Eaton, and Ilkeston.

One major TGWU figure was Muriel Rayment, of EMI in West Middlesex. A member of the Engineering National Trade Group Committee and later the GEC. She had taken a leading role in organizing women workers, and as the war approached its end, she was decisive in reminding the union of the missing link in the union's work – organizing women in Area 1. She was a nationally renowned campaigner in the fight for equal pay and workplace nurseries, with other leading lay women in the TGWU (then mostly communists) such as Peggy McIlven (Standard Telephone), Nell Coward (Liverpool Royal Ordnance Factory), Anne Wheeler (London), Flo Mitten (Manchester) and Peggy Stanton (Convenor, West London Aircraft). Molly Keith, a London bus conductress, was a leading figure in the struggle – an unassuming, hard-working, dedicated anti-fascist, who gave her life to the labour movement and never stopped fighting for women's equality.

Throughout 1942 the role of women in the TGWU became a major policy issue. Pleas for women to join the union were matched by calls for 'proper wages and conditions' for women workers. The TUC's women conference realized the need for long working hours but also debated the

12 TUC online history.

problems associated with such unsocial working. They were particularly incensed by the operation of the 'black market' whereby goods were pilfered and sold on to the detriment of those sticking to the rules. Deakin was a strong voice for women in the union, 'we demand fair play for women war workers' (*The Record*, October 1942). Florence Hancock argued for real improvements in the status of women at work and that pay should be based on the 'rate for the job'.

The TGWU convened its first women's conference in October. It was mainly concerned with equal pay, part-time work, and absenteeism (*The Record*, October 1943):

> Three hundred working women represented 300,000 woman members of the union from every sort of war industry [...] They pledged their wholehearted determination to fight the war to the bitter end. [...] Delegate after delegate raised their voices against sex discrimination in industry. They described the inequality of working on the same job as men but for less money as 'scandalous'. It resulted in resentment and was a drag on the war effort [...] Phyllis Mouston, who works in a Royal Ordnance factory, moved a resolution demanding the rate for the job which was carried unanimously[...] 'The time has arrived', said Miss Mouston 'to put an end once and for all to sex discrimination on wages. Employers must be nailed down to keep agreements. Far too many find a thousand and one loopholes to escape their obligations'. Miss I. Eidridge of London, a factory worker, hit squarely at the contention of some employers that women of 18 years of age are juniors. 'If at 18 women can have children and look after a home, then they are old enough to receive the rate for the job if they go to work in the factory'. Julia Turner, of Scotland, a transport worker, said her friends receive the rate for the job.

> [...] Miss Peggy McKay, a London bus conductress, observed that a considerable percentage of absenteeism is inevitable when mothers of families are working in industry without proper provision for their children [...]. She appealed to delegates to support the resolution – later carried unanimously – which called upon the union to fight against all unjustifiable absenteeism through the joint production committees or similar joint bodies. (*Daily Worker*, 8 October 1943)

Away from conferences, women continued to fight for the basics: pay in engineering and the vehicle repair industry, and against growing redundancies and the impact of demobilization in early 1945.

The TGWU had supported the general principle that workers in the colonies should be granted more rights and enjoy improvements in living standards. The emphasis was on the establishment of 'free' trade unions (on the British model) and genuine 'good faith' bargaining backed by legislation. In the autumn of 1939 Bevin spoke in New York advancing the Commonwealth model that 'allows for the blending of acute racial difficulties into a political whole' (*The Record*, September 1942). It was Creech Jones who was the main spokesman for the TGWU, and pushed the ideal of the 'new social order' to include all workers within the British Empire. He argued for a position 'with no race superiority, and no interest inequality between ourselves and the peoples'. This meant support for self-government, and backing of rights for Africans in Kenya, Rhodesia, and South Africa. He continued that in the West Indies 'there was an urgent need for more community education, and for an immediate tackling of the problems of economic organisation and production'. He called for the end to the 'old imperialism' but remained unclear as to the exact nature of the future, and this lack of concise analysis hindered him and the Labour government after the war when dealing with national independence movements (*The Record*, August 1942).

In 1943 the TGWU was represented by Dalgleish on the Colonial Labour Advisory Committee in which the good treatment of the 'natives' was to be a priority. As thoughts turned to the 'new social order' so international trade and the world's currency situation were increasingly debated by the TGWU. The TGWU leaders seemed out of their depth, but they were clearer on the relevance to their members of any future trade deals, especially ones based on 'mutual gains'. By the autumn of 1944 the TGWU, through Creech Jones, repeated its somewhat ambiguous stance, talking of colonial peoples having to 'rely on us' for their futures, and at the same time concerned with the starvation among the peoples of West Africa (*The Record*, September 1944).

In the run up to the 1945 general election, the TGWU was increasingly concerned to 'maintain Empire preference' in trade, and there were worries that the new world order of collective security might be threatened by our erstwhile allies, the Soviets. Some early signs of the Cold War could be seen in speeches by TGWU leaders saying they 'hoped Russia are still our friends' (*The Record*, June 1945). A central concern was Indian independence with labour movement support, but they fretted over the possibility of communist advances on the subcontinent before there was time to establish British-style institutions including trade unions.

'The New Social Order': Full Employment and Welfare

The banishing of the four horsemen of the apocalypse – conquest
(on a white horse); war (on a red horse); famine (on a black horse);
and death (on a pale horse).

The central change in policy terms was an acceptance that the state had to play a major role in the economic and social life of the nation. This meant taking responsibility for full employment as the basis for all welfare reforms and post-war reconstruction initiatives. These would be paid for from a national insurance scheme outlined in the Beveridge report, and welcomed by the TGWU leadership. The union leadership favoured some form of 'free collective bargaining' to allow wage adjustments to match costs, prices, and profits. This clashed with those supporting wartime compulsion in arbitration, and advocating its extension into the peace to come.[13]

The New Deal in American had already been running since 1933 and was a practical example of government spending to pull the economy, and especially jobs, out of the slump. When Keynes met Roosevelt, according to Galbraith, there was no meeting of minds – Keynes thought the president dense, and the president thought the English economist a wild-eyed theoretician.[14] Nonetheless, both in their own ways, restored the system through the basic expedient of government borrowing to spend on employment and investment. While the British government clung on to the last vestiges of laissez-faire, others were happy to embrace capitalist planning, sustained by piecemeal help to big business, to dig themselves out of the large hole created by the Great Crash.

In material terms it was the rise of the powerful large corporations that eroded the support for laissez-faire as a policy.[15] At the heart of the official position of the TGWU was this hope that the contradictions of capitalism could be overcome by state intervention within limits, and with planning replacing the chaos that created unemployment.[16] It was to be banished from the land of hope and glory.

This argument for public ownership, as the basis of the 'new order', was made to the TGWU BDC in Llandudno on 18 August 1941. With the death of Ben Tillet, a founding father of the dockers' union, in January 1943

13 James Jaffe, 'The Ambiguities of Compulsory Arbitration and the Wartime Experience of Order 1305', *Historical Studies in Industrial Relations*, 2003, vol.15, pp.1–25; Nina Fishman, 'A Vital Element in British Industrial Relations': A Reassessment of Order 1305, 1940–51', *Historical Studies in Industrial Relations*, 1999, vol.8, pp.43–86.
14 J.K. Galbraith, *The Age of Uncertainty* (1977), quoted from the BBC TV series.
15 Cole, *Economics*, p.14.
16 Leo Huberman, *Man's Worldly Goods* (Victor Gollancz, 1937).

at the age of 82, came a reminder of how far the TGWU had come but also how far it had to go to achieve the sort of socialism for which he had fought.

> The pressures for the state to own and manage public services fall into three main categories: evolutionary pragmatism rooted in the needs of a Britain which rapidly industrialized, urbanized, and then spread into a contentious Empire. A rightwing imperative of national renewal and control to save capitalism from itself, and a socialist imperative for justice for all citizens to live without fear.[17]

State intervention in the social and economic life of its citizens became both popular and accepted throughout the political spectrum. It was not until 1942, with the strong belief that whatever happened Britain would not fall to the Nazis, that practical schemes on reconstruction started to be debated. It was the commitment to full employment that mattered most. If there was full employment then, the TGWU leaders believed, there would be a win-win outcome: it would remove the scourge of unemployment, it would strengthen the bargaining position of the unions for better wages and conditions; and it would provide the opportunity for the TGWU to sit at the table with employers and the state representatives. In other words the union would come of age.

At the time this was both the policy intention and the practical outcome of the war years. While Keynes had provided the theoretical underpinning for the capitalist state to move away from the dominant dogma of laissez-faire, it was liberal social reformers and leaders of the labour movement that made it a concrete reality. Aspiration met reality in the heady days of 1945. The actual economics, while based on discussion of equilibrium theories, was good old-fashioned government borrowing to spend to modernize the economy. This would allow some of the new prosperity to fund health, welfare, and education free-for-all at the point of use. Deakin and Bevin embraced such solutions as exactly for what they had fought, and their members enthusiastically welcomed such reforms.

Citizens at large spoke of post-war reconstruction and this time they were determined not to be cheated. 'The most substantial of these rewards was a plan for universal social security, worked out by Sir William Beveridge. This fulfilled at last the Fabian plans laid down by the Webbs before the First World War'. It provided against poverty and unemployment [...] 'moreover, Beveridge, the Liberal planner, assumed the continued working of capitalism and finally rejected the socialist doctrine of a social security provided by society'.[18]

---

17   Roger Seifert, *Public Services: The Good, the Bad, and the Future* (CLASS, 2014), p.5.

18   Taylor, *English History*, p.567.

TGWU activists were cheered by this glimpse of a better future, and

No one believed more strongly than Bevin that, even in the middle of the war, it was right to think about the world that was to come out of it and that men and women would more willingly meet the demand for sacrifice and effort if they felt that these would contribute to making a juster and more equal society.[19]

The 'new social order' on offer was based on full employment and state ownership and control of parts of the economy. These were to form the foundation stones upon which universal social security (the term, 'the welfare state' was not used until after 1945),[20] and free health and education were to be built. There was the strongest determination among the general population that after this war, unlike the last war, government must deliver on its promises for a better society.

The aim was to be rid of poverty and unemployment. It was to be predicated upon the thriving modern capitalist economy and to be paid for through a flat-rate contribution unwittingly based on Lloyd George's 1911 compromise. 'Even so the Beveridge report seemed a great advance. In February 1943 the government gave it only faint blessing, Labour demanded more and revolted for the only time in the war'.[21]

The argument is that welfare in its various forms was derived from four sources: first, working-class experience and self-help; second, Marxist views on the role of the state in class society; third, a coalition of liberal reformers, socialist MPs and councillors; and fourth, the fear of revolt from below if nothing was done. Willie Gallacher argued that: 'the class struggle arising out of class relations was the means of giving workers the essential experiences for developing their organizations and formulating their political programmes'.[22] They feared, quite rightly, endless dilution of the most progressive aspects of the new world order and sabotage at every level as the reforms came on stream.

Deakin welcomed the Beveridge report and was delighted that it appeared to go further towards the TGWU's policies than expected. Here indeed was 'a prophet pointing the way to the Promised Land'.[23] The TGWU GEC understood that the report would have to be parked until the war was over. The report itself had a rocky start in Parliament and a group of Left MPs took it upon themselves to attack Bevin and other

19 Bullock, *Minister of Labour*, pp.76–77.
20 Asa Briggs, 'The Welfare State in Historical Perspective', *European Journal of Sociology*, 1961, vol.2, no.2, pp.221–258.
21 Taylor, *English History*, p.567.
22 William Gallacher, *Marxism and the Working Class* (Lawrence & Wishart, 1943), p.29.
23 Bullock (1967), *Minister of Labour*, p.226.

Labour ministers for their prevarication and lukewarm endorsement of the pillars and principles embedded in the reforms. Bevin's antagonism to the dissenters was based on a breach of their collective duty to back a coalition they had joined. The political realities seem to support another interpretation, namely his concern for the strength of the Left, their links with the communists, and the worries of opening a Pandora's Box of reforms.

In policy terms this meant an apparent muddle between Keynesian efforts to save capitalism by reforming it and the TGWU's policy of full employment by whatever means. In practice it was hardship aligned with socialist agitation that had won over the majority of citizens, and the political hegemony of Conservatism was dented for now. The TGWU welcomed all aspects of the report and reforms as a vindication of their policies and their new-found power in the land. The TGWU had fought and won the battle for the direction of reforms that was now on the table. At the top was full employment linked with state planning and ownership. This would aid the union's negotiations for better pay and conditions, provide job security, and allow the union's voice to be heard in the corridors of power.

Reconstruction now loomed large. Inside the PLP it was Bevan who took on his old adversary, Bevin. As Foot suggests, 'Bevin was supposed to be the hard-headed trade union leader, Bevan the impractical phrase-monger. But it was Bevan who did his best to bring Bevin down to earth'.[24] This point was part of a wider and deeper set of suspicions mooted by Bevan and his left allies towards the Conservative opposition to welfare reform, and Labour and the trade union Panglossian acceptance that 'all was for the best in the best of all possible worlds'. In this Bevin played a poor hand by siding with the leaders of the Coalition rather than with the Labour Party, and more importantly, with the unions and the working class he purported to personify. Bevin is presented as the man in the middle between socialists and laissez-faire capitalists: 'Bevin did not share either of these views: he was implacably opposed to any return to a nineteenth-century free enterprise capitalist society but had little faith in the immediate practicality of the socialist revolution'.[25]

The report was presented by its author, Sir William Beveridge, to the British Parliament in November 1942.[26] It provided a summary of principles necessary to banish poverty and abolish want. The paper proposed a system of social security which would be operated by the state, and implemented at war's end. It redefined poverty in terms of

24 Michael Foot, *Aneurin Bevan: Volume 1 1897–1945* (McGibbon & Key, 1962), pp.441–442.

25 Bullock, *Minister of Labour*, p.276.

26 *Social Insurance and Allied Services*, Cmd 6404.

subsistence living and set the tone for the debate on poverty itself and the levels of support required to reduce its absolute impact. The report's aim was to provide social insurance from the 'cradle to the grave' through a compulsory weekly contribution paid to the state in return for benefits claimed when unemployed, sick, widowed, and retired. The ideological underpinning was much more about sharing the risks of life's twists and turns rather than blaming them on idle fecklessness of the poor. The experiences of war and unemployment were the material bases for such shifts in attitudes.

In June 1943 the Labour Party officially adopted the Beveridge Plan as policy, but not without some angry debate. The TGWU gave its blessing to the scheme, warts and all, and decried opposition from left Labour MPs as opportunism

> Mr Arthur Deakin [...] supported the executive's resolution [to back Beveridge] [...] It was made clear by Sir William Beveridge that the scheme depended for its success on a high average of employment. There were several reasons why a number of Labour M.P.s voted against the Government, he said, and went on to name one of them as purely a piece of political expediency. Loud cries of 'No' greeted this. 'All right' said Mr. Deakin, 'I have my opinion and you can have yours'. Speak for your union' shouted a voice. 'I am speaking for my union', Mr. Deakin replied hotly. 'You are not'. returned a voice. 'I am the best judge of that', said Mr. Deakin. (*Daily Worker*, 16 June 1943)

The TGWU, on its twenty-first birthday, represented 1,122,480 members. This was also the time when the TUC formally withdrew the 'black circulars' from policy. In 1944 the momentum for unity of purpose was developing, particularly over post-war plans. The TUC conference in Blackpool in 1944 endorsed, with TGWU support, the interim report on post-war reconstruction – with planning and full employment centre stage. This included demands for public ownership, public control of industry, a National Industrial Council, price controls, and a National Investment Board. This was all linked to the desire for a World Trade Union Federation which had wide support despite American objections (*The Record*, March 1945).

Socialists of all hues welcomed the shift to state intervention and policy aims of full employment, nationalization, and welfare, but warned that it was not enough. They feared that much would be a temporary fix, and was not secure since capitalism remained largely unreformed. *The Resistible Rise of Arturo Ui* (by Bertolt Brecht, 1941) makes clear in parable form the ability of capitalism to reinvent itself. Left economists spoke of the 'illusions' on offer including that of 'full employment', noting that the reformers suggested that they had 'discovered the ways and means of abolishing mass unemployment – the central plague of capitalism – without in any way interfering with the foundations of the system itself'.[27] This theme runs through Marxist critiques of Keynesianism: 'This relative absence of unemployment undoubtedly made a deep and favourable impression on the British workers [...] It provided, in fact, a basis for many illusions'.[28] The importance of this counter-argument for the TGWU was that it differentiated between reform and revolution, between social democracy and socialism, and provided an alternative analysis that warned that full employment was a political question and not just one of technical economic innovation.[29] It informed leadership policy with a bridge to the Labour Party, and it also came to dominate TGWU education classes as the splits on the Left intensified during the Cold War.

The socialist Left saw it as a courageous attempt to create an 'efficient, unified system of social insurance', but it left untouched private ownership of production and the powerful monopolies. Special praise was given to aspects such as the creation of the NHS, injured workers' compensation schemes, and equal benefits for men and women. Most TGWU members shared this view, and looked forward to the better life on offer. It was a victory for working-class struggle, but it was not socialism. At times the TGWU leaders drifted into evangelical fervour about the future 'promised land' of 'milk and honey'. The 'celestial city', however, was to remain under capitalist control. At the 1943 BDC they said, 'the workers are heartily sick of private enterprise' and by Easter 1944 'we must plan on the basis of an expanded economy'. This coincided with the declaration from the Philadelphia Conference of the International Labour Organization (ILO) stating that 'labour is not a commodity', that poverty is a danger to everyone, that freedom of association is fundamental, and that 'the war against want' must be fought unrelentingly.[30] John Price gave the TGWU's full backing to both the letter and spirit of such declarations (*The Record*, June 1944).

The Bretton Woods conference in New Hampshire (USA) in July 1944 set up both the International Monetary Fund (IMF) and the International Bank for Reconstruction and Development (later part of the World Bank).[31] Keynes played a decisive role in the negotiations that

27 J.R. Campbell, *Some Economic Illusions in the Labour Movement* (Lawrence & Wishart, 1959), p.8.

28 Stephen Bodington writing as John Eaton, *Economics of Peace and War* (Lawrence & Wishart, 1952), p.8.

29 Sam Aaronovitch, *Economics for Trade Unionists* (Lawrence & Wishart, 1964).

30 Carter Goodrich, 'International Labor Conference of 1944', *Monthly Labor Review*, 1944, vol.58, no.3, pp.490–499.

31 Raymond Mikesell, 'Bretton Woods: Original Intentions and Current Problems', *Contemporary Economic Policy*, 2000, vol.18, no.4, pp.404–414.

Figure 5: Beveridge report
Credit: Marx Memorial
Library archive

were to shape the post-war international economic order. He led the British delegation to the conference which set out the institutional and policy requirements to prevent recession, and to reclaim the world for a more peaceful and prosperous future. It was here that the harsh realities of world trade came face to face with the promises made by the British labour movement to its members and followers. The TGWU leaders welcomed the general thrust of the agreement (*The Record*, August 1944), but appeared overly optimistic as to its implications for the stability of British trading arrangements.

All these 'good intentions' became de facto subordinated to US foreign policy. Despite the Keynesian tinge to the ideas with the avoidance of a second Great Slump, it was American Cold War policy that prevailed. The project, in terms of international currency stability and planned investments, failed as the ever-stronger dollar trumped all efforts to create an international community of interests.

It is telling that Kenneth Morgan starts his monumental study of post-war Britain with a quote from Beveridge. His remarks were rooted in 'the determination of the British democracy to look beyond victory to the uses of victory', to 'follow a people's war with a people's peace'.[32] There was the strongest sense that this time around the people would not allow their aspirations to be destroyed by government. It would indeed herald in 'the century of the common man' (*The Record*, September 1944).

The TGWU on the Brink of Peace: 'Somewhere over the Rainbow'[33]

With both the Soviets and Americans now directly involved in hostilities, the Allies slowly, and at enormous cost, gained ground over their hateful enemies. The war remained a national imperative and the coalition of political opinion stayed firm, with the anti-communism of the TGWU leadership in abeyance. Hard graft at home with workers working flat out for the war effort was matched by sacrifice on the war fronts. Millions of lives were lost and many more millions disrupted and put on hold. As the Allies inched ever closer to defeating the Germans on the Russian front, the Italians in their own backyard, and the Japanese in the far corners of the Far East, so thoughts turned to what a post-war world might look like. Significant and lasting policy shifts were being won with the notions of a free education service, an NHS of sorts, and planned economies to eliminate unemployment and develop growth. Many TGWU members, however, did not trust their own leaders or the leadership of the Labour Party to deliver. For now the second front was a major demand of the socialists throughout Europe, and the trades unions played their part once it had started. Deakin put his union into the wholehearted support for a second front, and made that a practical matter at home, congratulating the initiative shown by the JPC at Multitone Electric in London.

In March 1944 the government was at odds over reconstruction plans as popular opinion turned against the prevailing Conservative notions of building back better. Progressive ideals and practices had gained widespread support after years of argument and struggle. At the heart of this battle of ideas was the role of the state – more intervention, more planning, and more redistributive justice were demanded as a test of British democracy that could deliver to the majority the rewards of their sacrifices. The TGWU was at the front of the queue on all such issues, combining its social democratic realism with a dash of red sauce. More pragmatically, it urged its members to help evacuees from the flying

---

32 William Beveridge, *Pillars of Security* (George Allen & Unwin,1943) quoted in Kenneth Morgan, *Britain Since 1945: The People's Peace* (Oxford University Press, 1999), p.3.
33 Yip Harburg's song from *The Wizard of Oz*.

bombs, with Deakin personally exhorting his members to be generous in taking in those bombed out.

Underlining much of this was the issue of class. The Conservatives restated their claim to represent the privileged while Labour increasingly sought to form a coalition of the working classes writ large. It was the rise in strikes that became another litmus test of the links between the TGWU leadership and Bevin at the Ministry of Labour. In Northern Ireland, for example, major employers such as Harland and Wolff had over 30,000 on their books. The unions were dominated by skilled Protestant men. They were not shy in flexing their industrial muscle and in 1944 there were 252 strikes, including one in the Belfast shipyards over the imprisonment of five of their shop stewards.[34] On 8 April, the *Daily Worker* reported: 'THE release last night of the five aircraft workers serving terms of three months' imprisonment, for taking part in the Belfast strike, is likely to be the signal for 20,000 Belfast shipyard workers to return to work'.

Bevin attacked the strikers, and in early April he strengthened the penalties for those taking part in unofficial strikes. Bevan spoke on behalf of those trade unionists bitterly opposed to Bevin's carve-up with the employers and willing trade union leaders including Deakin. The accusation was that Bevin himself had orchestrated the witch-hunt against the strikers. Bevan also rallied against Order 1305 and its enforcement, and continued that leaders such as Deakin were out of touch with rank-and-file opinion across the nation.

This increasing pressure from below was partly associated with low unemployment and a stronger position for workers around the bargaining table.

Men and women who had endured years without work or had lived under the permanent threat of unemployment obviously welcomed the favourable wartime conditions. By June 1944 the unemployed numbered only 54,000 or 0.7 per cent of the employable population. The war not only guaranteed work for all fit enough to do it but also provided plenty of overtime to those in vital industries. As a consequence, average earnings increased by 80 per cent, whereas prices only rose 60 per cent between 1939 and 1945. Many, however, saw war work as little more than a brief respite from poverty. As they believed mass unemployment would return with the peace, workers struck for higher wages while they could.[35]

34 Philip Ollerenshaw, 'War, Industrial Mobilisation and Society in Northern Ireland, 1939–1945', *Contemporary European History*, 2007, vol.16, no.2, pp.169–197.
35 Steven Fielding, 'The Good War' in Nick Tiratsoo (ed.), *From Blitz to Blair* (Phoenix, 1997), pp.37–38.

The war conditions for workers on the buses and in passenger transport remained tough. At the Annual Passenger Conference on 8 December 1942, for example, they pushed for an increase in wages for both men and women. The next conference on 29 December 1943 expressed the hope that new members, mainly women, would stay in the union after the war had ended and keep fighting to build the union movement (*The Record*, January 1944).

The general workers trade group in the TGWU also recorded a huge increase in women members through the expansion of factory jobs. These included those making glass, plaster board, café workers, general engineering, and pressed steel. In most cases shop stewards were quickly appointed and in larger workplaces a branch was established. Even so difficulties were never far away, and there were increasing reports of unhelpful management (in garages, laundries), and as women fought and won pay parity (as in the Cerebos Salt works) there was some resentment among their male colleagues, as with the 'packing squads' who packed the salt into containers for transport. Reports from 1943 indicate some efforts by management to push back on equal pay for women through the tired expedient of job regrading (Royal Ordnance Factory Spennymoor). Members in the RTP section remained 'unhappy' as there was some job loss and little movement on wages.

By early 1945 more redundancies and reduced overtime working meant falling living standards for some TGWU members, with little support from the centre. There was an accelerating rate of lay-offs in factories and government departments. Among members, therefore, the notion of full employment as the basis for the 'brave new world' seemed less than realistic. In June 1945 the TGWU published a booklet, *Your Union. How it works and what it seeks to do* (*The Record*, June 1945). This was an effort to revitalize somnolent branches, re-energize activists, re-awaken area officials and committees, and above all to persuade new members to stay in the union.

Later that April, Bevin addressed the annual TGWU festival in Bristol. He attacked Bevan and took up his usual victim role – becoming the butt of unjustified accusations of being a reactionary. *Tribune* on 5 May 1944 replied: 'a free vote throughout the Trade Union movement would [...] dispose utterly of the claim of Mr Ernest Bevin [...] to speak as the Labour Emperor whose slightest whims are honoured law among the working people of this land'. Bevan himself was clear that the right-wing of the Labour Party backed by the leadership of the TUC and TGWU wanted to continue an alliance with big business and friendly Tories after the war.[36]

36 Foot, *Bevan*, p.461.

This political grouping supported a modern approach to ownership, management, government regulation, and the harnessing of the new technologies. They wanted full employment to be at the centre of such developments and again Deakin and the TGWU GEC were willing allies. Some of the contradictions of such reforms became apparent – private enterprise was insisted upon as part of the dynamic needed for investment and innovation, but state planning was required as well to direct such enterprises to where they were most needed in areas of traditional depression. The policy sought to merge the two tendencies into what was later known as indicative planning, favoured in the corporatism of post-war France and Germany.

An example involving the TGWU was the suggestion for an expanded dock development on the Tees to replace the piecemeal existing private activities. The muddle was that the private sector should be given first refusal on such a state-initiated project, and failing that, some corporate board involving public funds and local authority controls would step in. Underpinning all was full employment and the final draft of the White Paper (May 1944, Cmd. 6527) dealing with the transition to peacetime labour market controls. Deakin in particular saw the need for pragmatism in the search for full employment, and openly eschewed any notion that socialism might be the only permanent answer. The rift was clear and lines were drawn in the sand that quickly became the hallmark of the bitter divisions inside the labour movement. The liberation of Paris and the Red Army's advance into Poland overshadowed all other news at home and abroad.

While the various national insurance bills were being debated in Parliament in the autumn of 1944, the Labour Party announced the end of the coalition government would come with the end of the war. Once it was clear that the next general election would be fought along party lines, those lines had to be drawn up. Here the powerful voice and deep pockets of the TGWU played its part. The union embraced the slogans 'forward with Labour' and 'labour stands united' with great enthusiasm (*The Record*, April 1945; *The Record*, June 1945).

Housing was already a major issue before the V1 and V2 attacks on London. The central divide was between state planning and ownership of the stock of new houses to be built with state aid, against the state providing the favourable conditions under which a private housebuilding boom could flourish. In both cases there was work for building workers and those involved in the supply chain. The TGWU leaders, rightly concerned for their own members, took the view that whatever the ways and means, any housing expansion was to be welcomed. Here the knotty question of controlled demobilization was central, and those interested parties involved broke ranks and pitted men and against women, and returning soldiers against current employees. The hope was that post-war expansion would find jobs for all (*The Record*, December 1944).

Age and length of service were the main basis for the order of demobilization with the main exception men (Class B) needed for reconstruction work, mainly housebuilding and repair. Part of this process also made special provision for the disabled, an issue close to the heart of the TGWU leaders (*The Record*, March 1944). Herbert Morrison's calls for a national plan for capital investment and technical advance in October 1944 met with a mixed reception from inside the labour movement. The socialist elements of the proposals worried some as making the Party unelectable, others on the Left saw them as too vague and limited, and others from the trade union side wanted jobs and better pay from whatever source. The debate, arcane at the time, was about the form state ownership would take. This was about both the exact nature of the ownership model and the management of such vast enterprises. In the end the top-down and top-heavy Morrisonian model won the day, with dire consequences for their later success.

Such matters were overwhelmed by events outside these shores. With the German retreat and Soviet advance in Europe came the issue of future self-determination for each liberated sovereign state. In Greece, where the local communists were strong, Churchill ordered British troops to fight against the resistance to prevent a communist take-over. This was met with outrage as it meant that the British army was fighting with and for Greeks who had sided with the Nazis. Here the Labour Party leadership showed once again their limitations by seeking a compromise rather than out-and-out condemnation of such partisan use of troops. Bevin persuaded the TGWU leadership to back the compromise and avoid openly attacking Churchill's decision, and once again the TGWU leaders fell into line. For the sake of unneeded unity for the coalition government the trade union and Labour Party leaders failed to match their rhetoric about freedom and democracy. This set the tone for much of the foreign policy of the 1945 Labour government under Bevin's control as foreign secretary, and its anti-communist witch-hunts at home. Here was ideology dressed up as hard-headed realism, and anti-communism presented as pragmatism.

'We'll meet again, don't know where, don't know when ...'

At the Yalta meetings, from the 4–11 February 1945, the USSR and USA became closer as both wanted a rapid end to the war in Europe and the Far East, while a weaker UK government was already wary of too much Soviet triumph. Churchill, true to form, was mainly concerned to prevent a communist clean sweep of liberated territories. In contrast Roosevelt was much more sanguine about any Soviet gains. Churchill thus sought to recapture some lost ground with the 14 February 1945 blanket bombing of Dresden to weaken German morale. All this changed to the British advantage when on 12 April 1945 Roosevelt died, to be replaced by the less popular and more anti-Soviet Truman. The war in Europe was rapidly coming to its conclusion when on 28 April Mussolini was executed, and two days later Hitler killed himself.

On 7 May 1945, unconditional surrender by Germany was announced and Victory in Europe (VE) day was 8 May. The last meeting of the big three wartime allies was held at the end of July in Potsdam, after which Truman took an aggressive anti-Soviet line and launched the Cold War. On 6 August (Hiroshima) and 9 August (Nagasaki), atomic bombs were dropped on Japan killing about 250,000 people immediately. Victory over Japan (VJ) day was 15 August 1945. Such a terrible end to such a terrible conflict brought hope and despair in a mixed bag of fortunes for winners and losers alike.

The coalition government was weakened and fragmented over its immediate future and the labour movement was forging unity to win the election while seeking to establish new policies to match the new world order. The TGWU strongly backed a raft of favourable legislation on wages and holiday pay. The key principle was the statutory regulations of wages and conditions of employment in sectors where the home-grown institutions were not up to the job of balanced collective bargaining. The main mechanism was the authority vested in independent boards, with members from the unions and employers setting hourly rates and guaranteed weekly wages. The voluntary tradition of collective bargaining was alive and well in the minds of trade union leaders such as Deakin, but not in reality.

The coalition ended on 23 May 1945. The TGWU openly urged all its members to vote Labour and campaigned accordingly (*The Record*, June 1945). At the election Labour offered what voters wanted: housing, employment, and social security. The result was a Labour landslide – 393 Labour MPs, 213 Conservatives, 12 Liberals, and 22 Independents were elected. Attlee became the first Labour prime minister of a majority government on 26 July. He appointed Bevin as foreign secretary, Dalton as the chancellor, and Bevan at health.

The country was in a financial mess, and rapidly fell under USA patronage. The British were the only people to fight both world wars from start to finish: 'Imperial greatness was on the way out; the welfare state was on the way in. The British Empire declined; the condition of the people improved'.[37]

The TGWU leaders were not that enthusiastic about continued state regulation as they believed the post-war boom would allow them to make gains through normal bargaining channels, especially in their strongholds. On the other side of the labour supply debate was the view that once the troops were back home they should be allowed to seek jobs

37 Taylor, *English History*, p.600.

freely, thus putting pressure on wages in some industries. In contrast the statists among the union leaders wanted controls to remain so that certain groups, the disabled and the young, could find work through state direction. TGWU members were wary of both and were more interested in safeguarding jobs and wages, and forcing through better training and apprenticeship schemes.

Many areas of the TGWU geared up for peacetime working patterns and further disruption. At this moment so much was down to local wrinkles in the systems that shop stewards tended to handle most of the action. In shipbuilding and ship repairing, for example, all problems were dealt with by the yard stewards.[38] As redundancies mounted up with the end of the war, union activists were fearful of mass lay-offs and loss of members and influence. The government made promises about directing investment to weaker areas such as the North East, but there was no concerted effort at planning and state involvement.

The war had altered women's role in society for ever and had enabled the workers in the colonies to expect and taste forms of self-government. Murray suggests 'from the neglected and oppressed margins of society, trade unions had risen to become an acknowledged power in the land, entrenched throughout industrial life, and had now secured an electoral landslide for their own political party'.[39]

At the end of the war in Europe and in the Far East the economy was in crisis. There were great debts, mass loss of workers from staple industries such as coal and textiles, and 'English people expected and deserved immediate improvements in their living conditions after the hardships of the war. At the very lowest, new houses and new clothes could not be delayed'.[40] Over 400,000 were killed (300,000 in the armed forces, 60,000 civilians, and 35,000 from the merchant navy) but the employed population was three million greater than in 1939. Critical to this was the growth of new industrial sectors: electricity, cars, iron and steel, nylons, machine tools, and chemicals. Rich pickings for the TGWU in the brave new world to come.

38 Minutes of General Workers Trade Group, 27 March 1945, Tyne and Wear Area; Tyne and Wear archives.
39 Murray, *T&G Story*, p.91.
40 Taylor, *English History*, p.599.

Conclusions

Jim Mortimer, speaking at the tenth anniversary of the Institute of Employment Rights (IER), repeated the central purpose of trade unionism: 'the development and extension of collective bargaining in all areas of employment is essential to promote social advance and to ensure that working people share in the benefits of economic progress'.[1] This was the core policy throughout the TGWU. In every area and in every industrial group, the union, at every level, strove to engage with employers in collective bargaining on behalf of their members. They favoured permanent formal joint councils and committees where possible. If this failed then they sought state intervention to guarantee basic terms and conditions.

The achievements of the TGWU in these long difficult years included a much stronger union organization, better pay and conditions, more resilient negotiating machinery, more state regulation, greater equality, and despite mass unemployment and world war, there was now hope. As the practicalities of post-war reconstruction unfolded, there were renewed fears over inflation, and with that came calls for wage controls to match price stability. The pressure from below, from militant union activists fighting for better wages, upset the TGWU apple cart of reasonable and responsible trade unionism.

The Beveridge Plan at the time, and ever since, has been the touchstone of the difference between socialists of various types and social democrats and liberal reformers. The latter embraced the report with great enthusiasm as a popular and necessary modernizing adjustment to the old social order. They were joined by those representing big business who also welcomed the principles of greater state involvement and greater equality as a means to create a highly profitable and stable post-war world. 'Beveridge seemed to have turned the public's vaguely

---

1 Jim Mortimer, *In Defence of Trade Unionism* (IER, 1998), p.9.

formulated desires for reform into a concrete programme'.[2] The 1945 general election vindicated this stream of political and social awareness, and Labour tapped into the national mood.

The leadership of the TGWU were delighted by this realization of their policies hammered out over years of debate. The entire spectrum of Left views came together to support the birth of the welfare state proper, but while the socialists saw it as a step in the right direction, the reformists regarded it as the end product of their campaigns. The TGWU wanted all and more with a seat for them at every bargaining table. But what they took with one hand they threw away with the other – too many concessions to big business, too many half-way houses with the Labour Party, and too much belief in Britain's trading prowess even as the Empire was ending and the Americans were coming.

Ron Todd (TGWU general secretary, 1985–1992) argued, 'for an organisation like ours, it has always made sense to examine where we have been, before asking where it is best to go now'.[3] The history of the trade union movement, of workers' struggles as members of the working class, is part of all history. It is 'a dialogue between the events of the past and progressively emerging future ends'.[4] This Enlightenment perspective on interpretation underlined the relevance of the historians' task, 'what they [Florentine historians of the early 1500s] most desired was, that their view of the course of events should have as wide and deep a practical effect as possible'.[5]

There is sufficient material in both oral and written forms to allow historians to put together an account of trade unions, trade unionism, and most importantly, the deeds of their members. This six-volume 'official' history of the TGWU, commissioned by Unite, will both pass and fail many of the tests set by others looking at such endeavours. The headline purpose must be not just to interpret and record the world, but to change it.

This volume of the TGWU's history has traced its growth and development from a somewhat ramshackle hit-and-miss affair in the early 1930s, through the tough times of unemployment and hostile governments, to a conclusion in 1945 where the union's general secretary was Minister of Labour, the union was the largest in the land, its finances and administration were in some sort of order, it had developed a fully-fledged education programme, and its reputation for representation and bargaining for all its members – men and women, young and old, skilled and semi-skilled, white collar and manual, Scottish, Welsh, Irish and English – was high. It was

2 Field, *Blood, Tears, and Toil*, p.337.

3 Ron Todd, Foreword to Ken Coates and Tony Topham, *The Making of the TGWU: The Emergence of the Labour Movement 1870–1922* (Blackwell, 1990), p.xvii.

4 E.H. Carr, *What is History?* (Pelican 1961), p.123.

5 Jacob Burkhardt (1860) *The Civilization of the Renaissance in Italy* (Phaidon Press, 1960), p.148.

a power in the land. And so the people's peace, that followed the people's war, delivered many, but not all, of the demands of the members of the TGWU forged in these struggles and made real in the political settlement of 1945...

Conclusions: Questions for Discussion

- How did the war alter attitudes to women workers?
- Why did the TGWU leadership support the Empire?
- Which shop-floor practices most aided the war effort?
- What did state intervention illustrate in terms of a planned economy?
- From where did plans for the welfare state originate?

Conclusions-Questions for Discussion

Index

Page numbers in **bold** refer to figures.